1980s ROCK

33 TOP GUITAR HITS OF THE DECADE

ISBN 978-1-4234-8932-0

HAL•LEONARD®
CORPORATION
7777 W. BLUEMOUND RD. P.O. BOX 13819 MILWAUKEE, WI 53213

For all works contained herein:
Unauthorized copying, arranging, adapting, recording, Internet posting, public performance,
or other distribution of the printed music in this publication is an infringement of copyright.
Infringers are liable under the law.

Visit Hal Leonard Online at **www.halleonard.com**

STRUM AND PICK PATTERNS

This chart contains the suggested strum and pick patterns that are referred to by number at the beginning of each song in this book. The symbols ⊓ and ⌄ in the strum patterns refer to down and up strokes, respectively. The letters in the pick patterns indicate which right-hand fingers plays which strings.

p = thumb
i = index finger
m = middle finger
a = ring finger

For example; Pick Pattern 2
is played: thumb - index - middle - ring

Strum Patterns   ## Pick Patterns

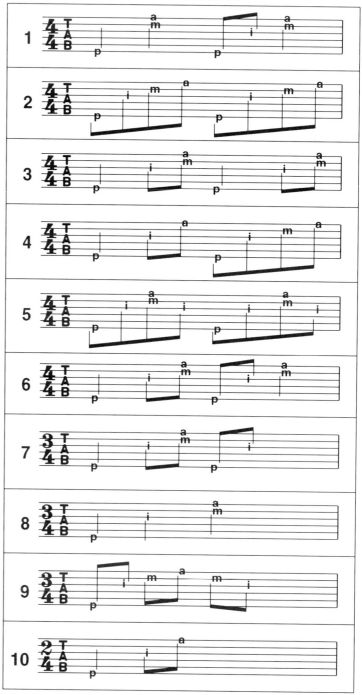

You can use the 3/4 Strum or Pick Patterns in songs written in compound meter (6/8, 9/8, 12/8, etc.).
For example, you can accompany a song in 6/8 by playing the 3/4 pattern twice in each measure.
The 4/4 Strum and Pick Patterns can be used for songs written in cut time (¢) by doubling the note time values in the patterns. Each pattern would therefore last two measures in cut time.

Call Me

from the Paramount Motion Picture AMERICAN GIGOLO

Words by Deborah Harry
Music by Giorgio Moroder

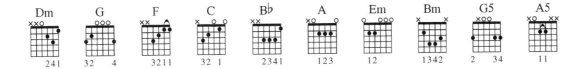

Strum Pattern: 1
Pick Pattern: 2

Intro
Fast Rock

Verse

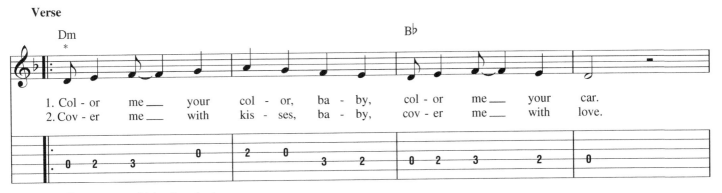

*Sung one octave higher throughout.

1. Col - or me __ your col - or, ba - by, col - or me __ your car.
2. Cov - er me __ with kis - ses, ba - by, cov - er me __ with love.

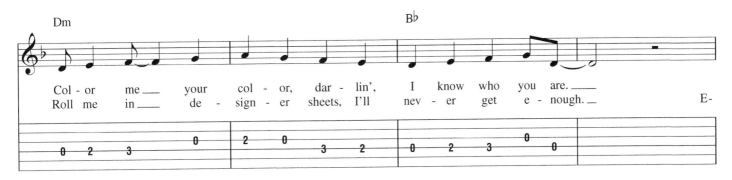

Col - or me __ your col - or, dar - lin', I know who you are. __
Roll me in __ de - sign - er sheets, I'll nev - er get e - nough. __

Copyright © 1980 Sony/ATV Music Publishing LLC, Chrysalis Music and Monster Island Music
All Rights on behalf of Sony/ATV Music Publishing LLC Administered by Sony/ATV Music Publishing LLC, 8 Music Square West, Nashville, TN 37203
All Rights on behalf of Monster Island Music Administered by Chrysalis Music
International Copyright Secured   All Rights Reserved

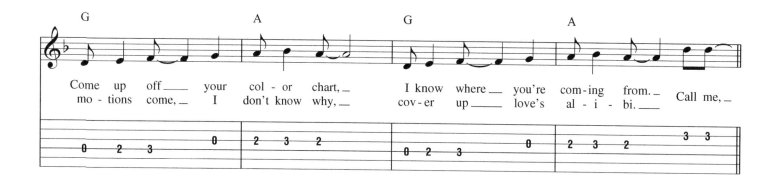

Come up off___ your col-or chart,___ I know where___ you're com-ing from.___ Call me,___
mo-tions come,___ I don't know why,___ cov-er up___ love's al-i-bi.___

Chorus

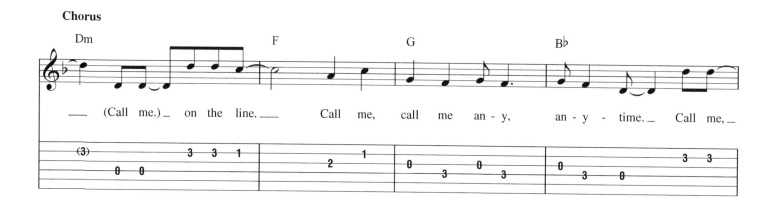

___ (Call me.)___ on the line.___ Call me, call me an-y, an-y-time.___ Call me,___

___ (Call me.)___ I'll ar-rive,___ you can call me an-y day___ or night.
when you're read-y we can___ share the wine. Call

me.

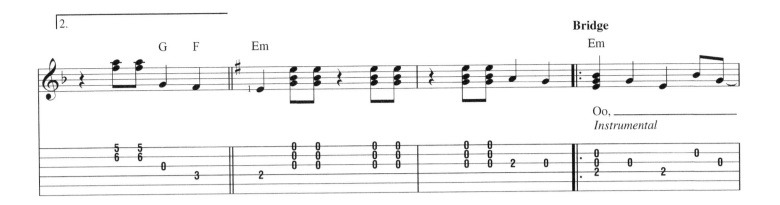

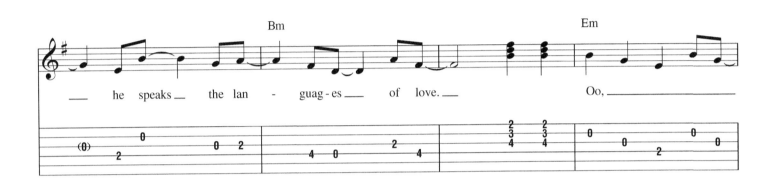

*Lyrics in italics are spoken.

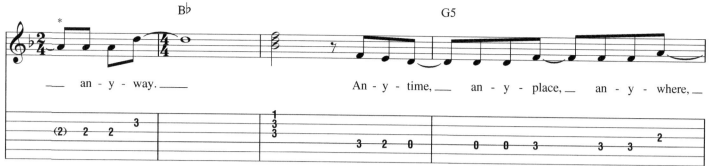

*Use Pattern 10.

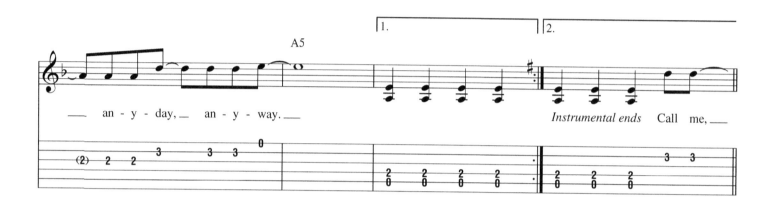

Chorus

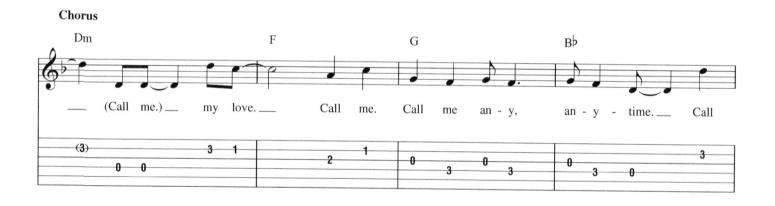

Outro-Chorus

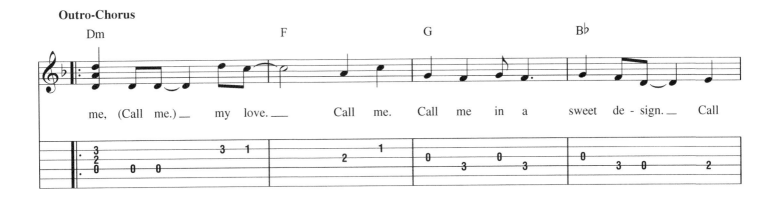

me, (Call me.) __ my love. ___ Call me. Call me in a sweet de - sign. __ Call

me. (Call me.) __ Call me for your lov - er's lov - er's al - i - bi. __ Call

me, (Call me.) __ in our life. ___ Call me. Call me an - y, an - y - time. __ Call

Repeat and fade

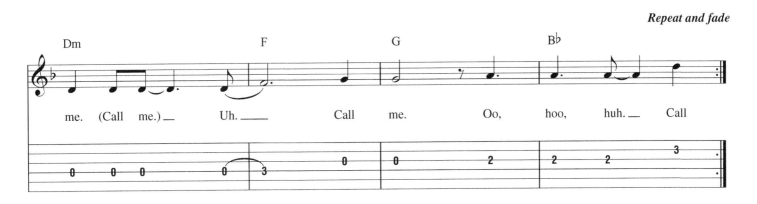

me. (Call me.) __ Uh. ___ Call me. Oo, hoo, huh. __ Call

Angel Eyes

Words and Music by John Hiatt and Fred Koller

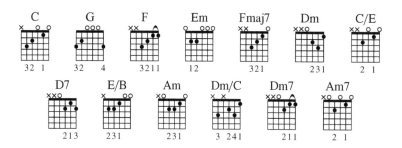

Strum Pattern: 2, 3
Pick Pattern: 2, 3

Intro
Slow Rock Ballad, in 2

𝄋 Verse

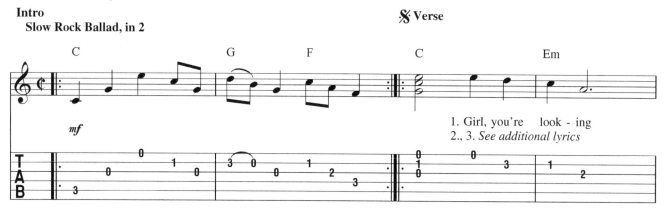

1. Girl, you're look - ing
2., 3. *See additional lyrics*

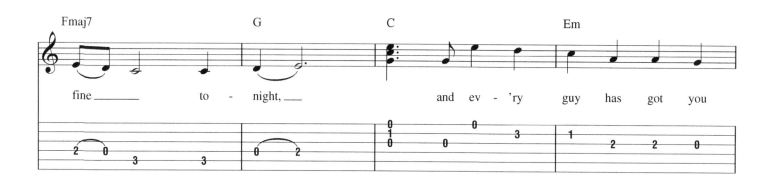

fine ___ to - night, ___ and ev - 'ry guy has got you

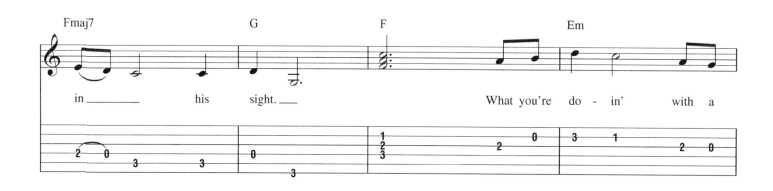

in ___ his sight. ___ What you're do - in' with a

Copyright © 1989 by Universal Music - Careers and Lucrative Music/Administered by Bug Music
International Copyright Secured   All Rights Reserved

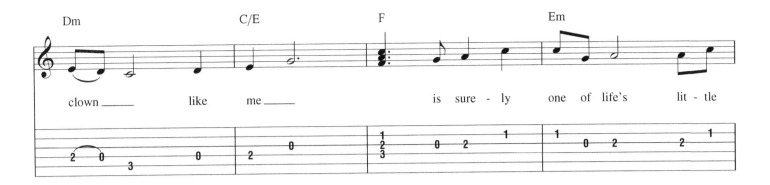

clown _____ like me _____ is sure - ly one of life's lit - tle

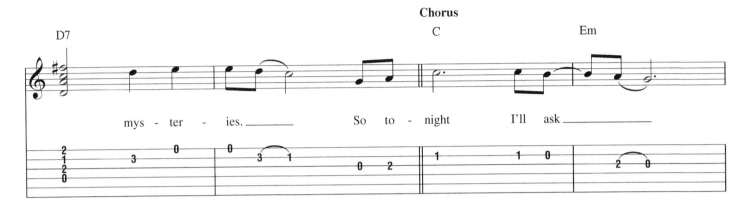

Chorus

mys - ter - ies. _____ So to - night I'll ask _____

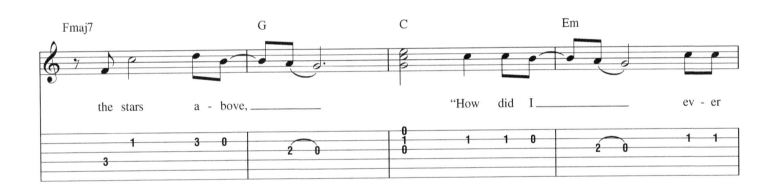

the stars a - bove, _____ "How did I _____ ev - er

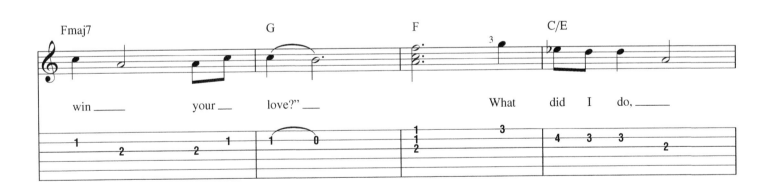

win _____ your _____ love?" _____ What did I do, _____

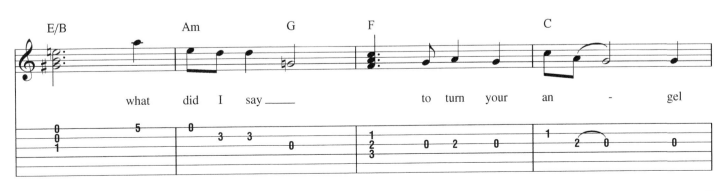

what did I say _____ to turn your an - gel

Additional Lyrics

2. Well, I'm the guy who never learned to dance.
   Never even got one second glance.
   Across a crowded room was close enough.
   I could look, but I could never touch.

3. Um, there's just one more thing I need to know:
   If this is love, why does it scare me so?
   It must be something only you can see,
   'Cause girl, I feel it when you look at me.

Bark at the Moon

Words and Music by Ozzy Osbourne

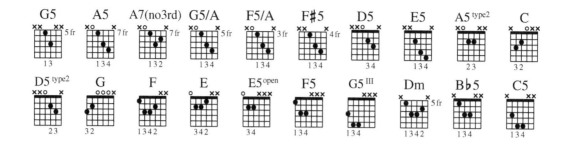

Strum Pattern: 2

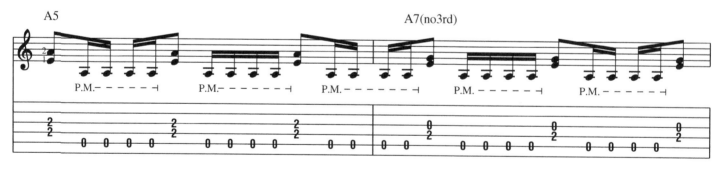

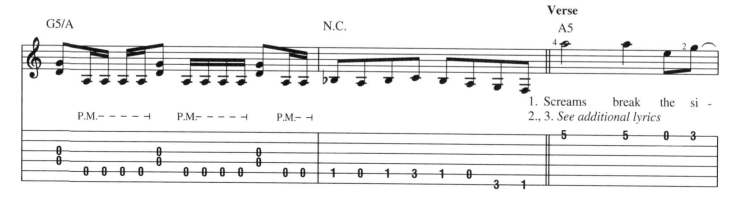

1. Screams break the si-
2., 3. *See additional lyrics*

© 1983 EMI VIRGIN MUSIC LTD.
All Rights for U.S.A. and Canada Controlled and Administered by EMI VIRGIN MUSIC, INC.
All Rights Reserved   International Copyright Secured   Used by Permission

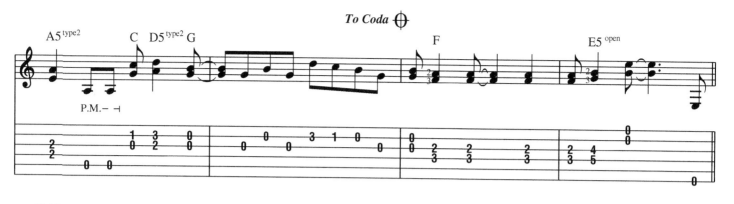

To Coda

Bridge
Half-time feel

They cursed and bur - ied him a - long with _____ shame ___

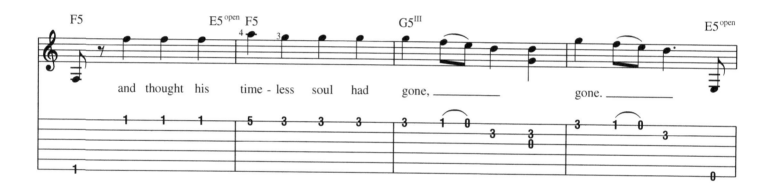

and thought his time - less soul had gone, _____ gone. _____

In emp - ty burn - ing hell, un - ho - ly _____ one, ___

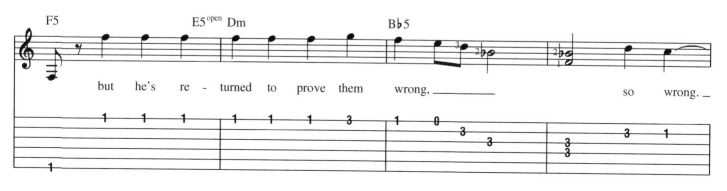

but he's re - turned to prove them wrong, _____ so wrong. ___

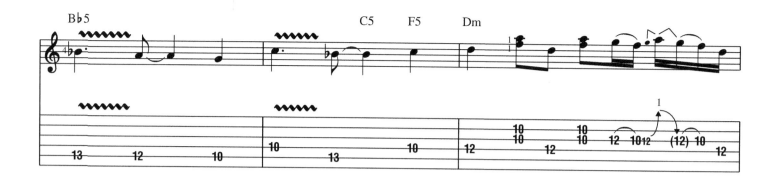

D.S. al Coda

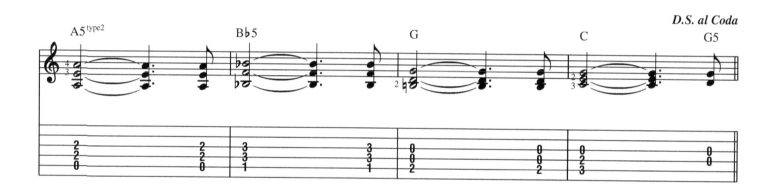

⊕ **Coda**

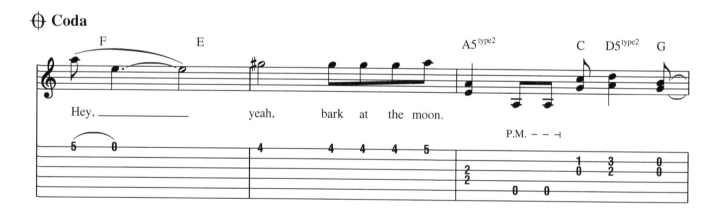

Hey, _____ yeah, bark at the moon.

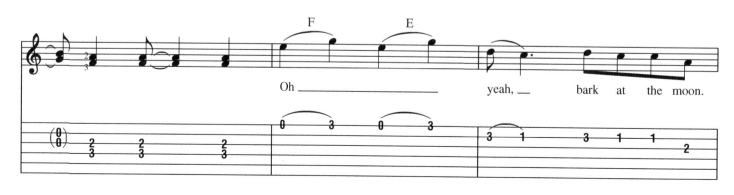

Oh _____ yeah, __ bark at the moon.

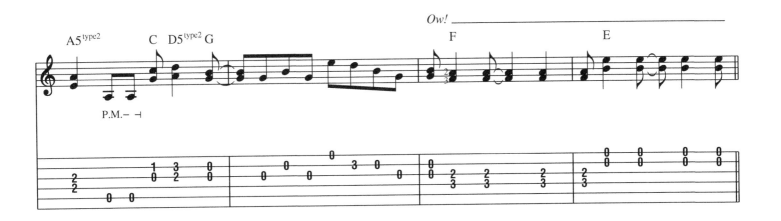

Outro

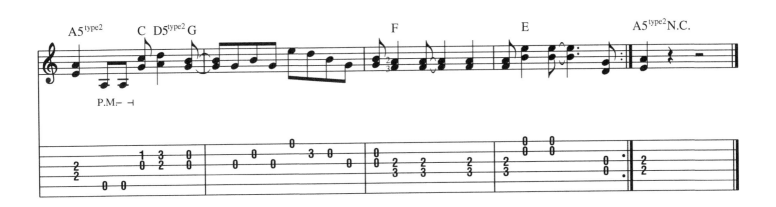

Additional Lyrics

2. Years spent in torment,
   Buried in a nameless grave.
   Now he has risen.
   Miracles would have to save.

Pre-Chorus 2., 3. Those that the beast is looking for,
   Listen in awe and you'll hear him
   Bark at the moon.

3. Howling in shadows,
   Living in a lunar spell.
   He finds his heaven
   Spewing from the mouth of hell.

Centerfold

Written by Seth Justman

Strum Pattern: 2, 5
Pick Pattern: 1, 4

© 1981 CENTER CITY MUSIC (ASCAP)/Administered by BUG MUSIC and PAL-PARK MUSIC
All Rights for PAL-PARK MUSIC Administered by ALMO MUSIC CORP.
All Rights Reserved   Used by Permission

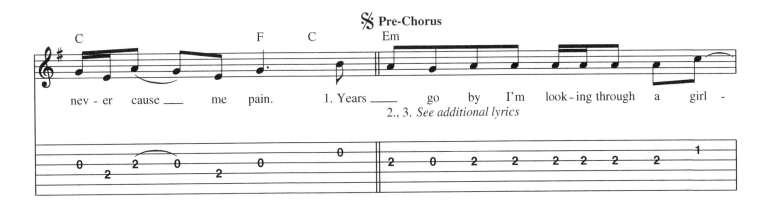

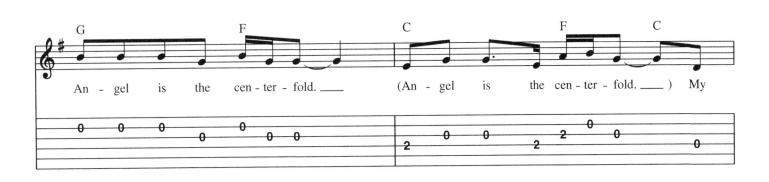

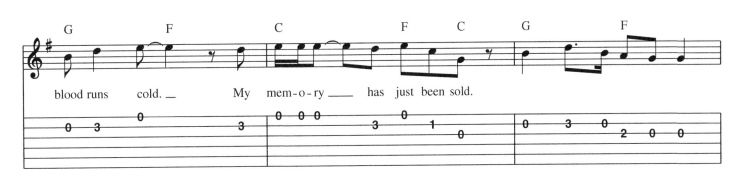

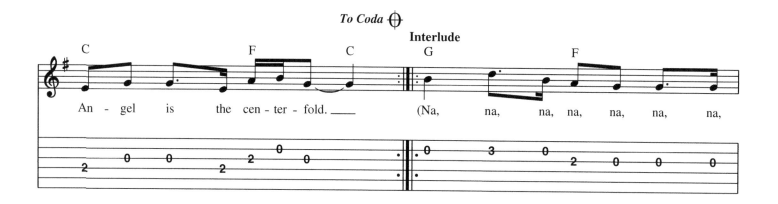

To Coda ⊕

Interlude

An - gel is the cen - ter - fold. ____ (Na, na, na, na, na, na, na,

|1., 2., 3.

|4.

na, na, na, na, na, na, na, na, na. na, na, na, na, na, na, na.)

Spoken: Now listen.

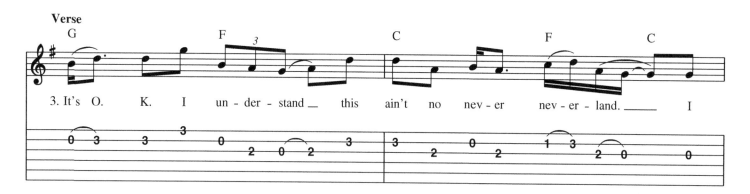

Verse

3. It's O. K. I un - der - stand _ this ain't no nev - er nev - er - land. ____ I

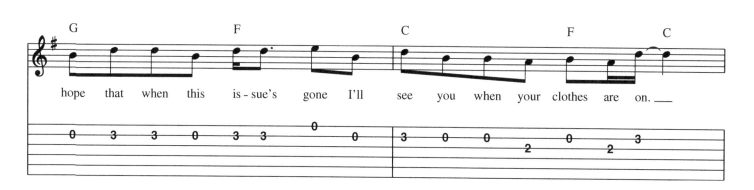

hope that when this is - sue's gone I'll see you when your clothes are on. __

Take your car, yes we will, _ we'll take your car and drive _ it. We'll

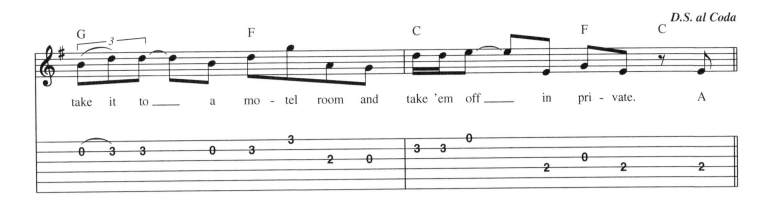

take it to ___ a mo-tel room and take 'em off ___ in pri - vate.   A

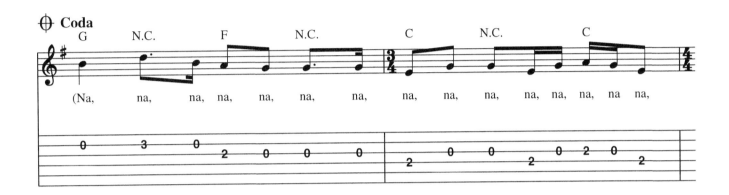

Coda

(Na,   na,   na, na,   na,   na,   na,   na,   na,   na,   na, na, na,   na   na,

Outro   *Repeat and fade*

Spoken: Al-right, al-right. One, two, three, four.
na. _____)   (Na,   na,   na, na, na, na,   na, na, na, na, na, na, na, na, na, na.)

Additional Lyrics

2. Slipped me notes under the desk
   While I was thinking about her dress.
   I was shy, I turned away,
   Before she caught my eye.
   I was shaking in my shoes
   Whenever she flashed those baby blues.
   Something had a hold on me when Angel passed close by.

Pre-Chorus 2. Those soft and fuzzy sweaters,
   Too magical to touch.
   To see her in that negligee
   Is really just too much.

3. A part of me had just been ripped,
   The pages from my mind are stripped.
   Oh no, I can't deny it.
   Oh yeah, I guess I gotta buy it.

Crazy Little Thing Called Love

Words and Music by Freddie Mercury

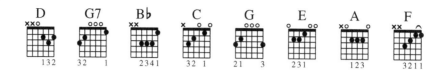

Strum Pattern: 1
Pick Pattern: 3

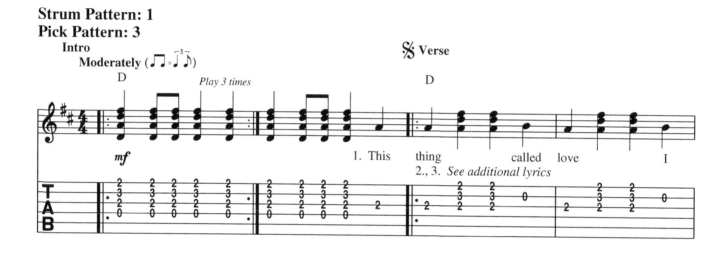

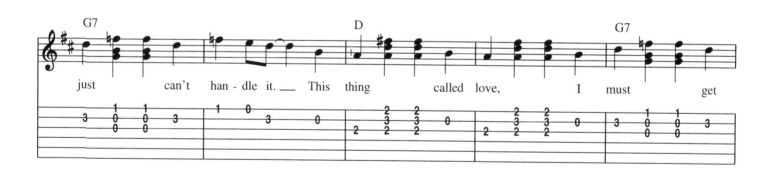

© 1979 QUEEN MUSIC LTD.
All Rights for the U.S. and Canada Controlled and Administered by BEECHWOOD MUSIC CORP.
All Rights for the world excluding the U.S. and Canada Controlled and Administered by EMI MUSIC PUBLISHING LTD.
All Rights Reserved   International Copyright Secured   Used by Permission

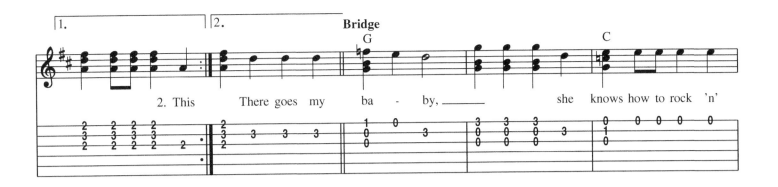

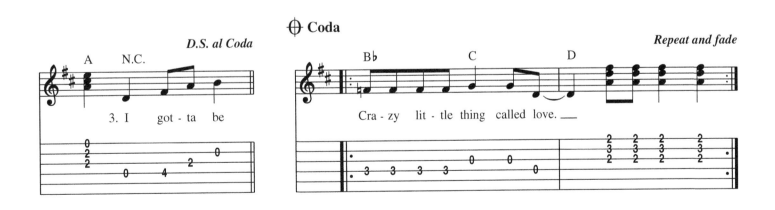

Additional Lyrics

2. This thing called love,
   It cries (like a baby) in a cradle all night.
   It swings, it jives,
   It shakes all over like a jellyfish.
   I kinda' like it.
   Crazy little thing called love.

3. I gotta be cool, relax,
   Get hip, get on my tracks.
   Take a backseat, hitchhike,
   And take a long ride on my motor bike
   Until I'm ready.
   Crazy little thing called love.

Don't Change

Words and Music by Andrew Farriss, Jon Farriss, Tim Farriss, Garry Beers, Michael Hutchence and Kirk Pengilly

Strum Pattern: 3, 5
Pick Pattern: 1, 3

Intro

Fast Rock

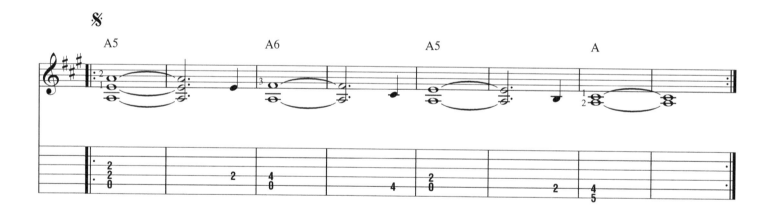

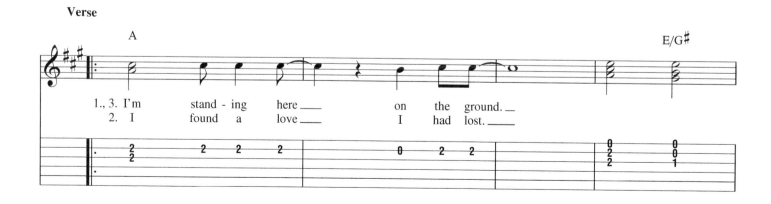

Copyright © 1982 MICHAEL BROWNING MUSIC MGMT. PTY. LTD.
All Rights in the U.S. and Canada Controlled and Administered by UNIVERSAL MUSIC CORP. and SONGS OF UNIVERSAL, INC.
All Rights Reserved   Used by Permission

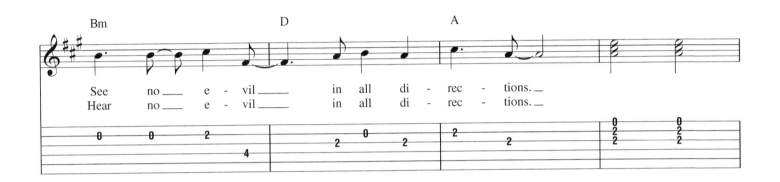

Chorus

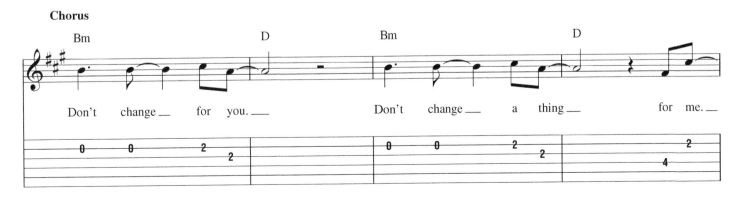

Don't change — for you. —

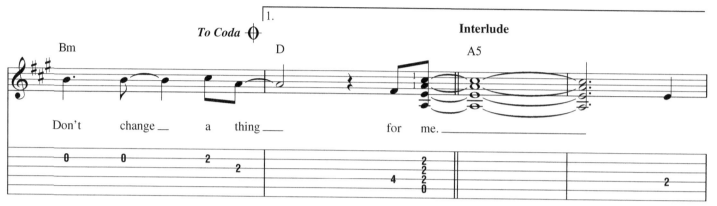

Don't change — a thing — for me.

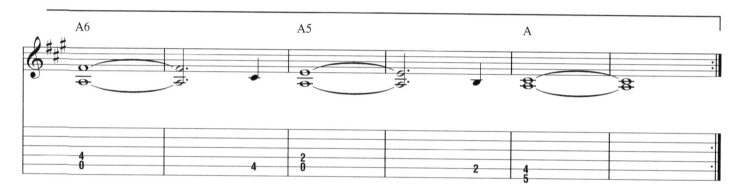

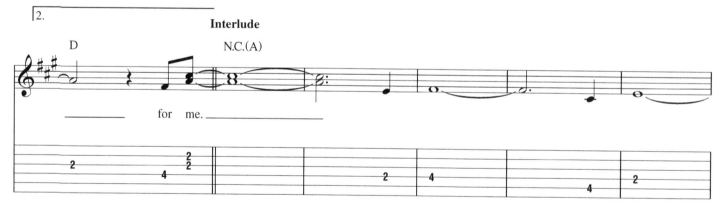

_____ for me. _____

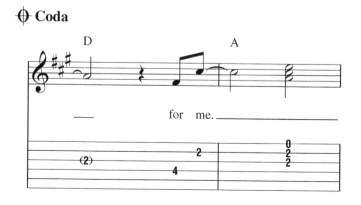

— for me. _____

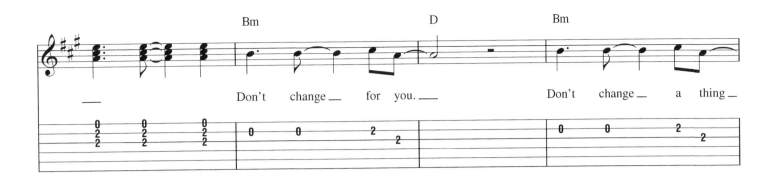

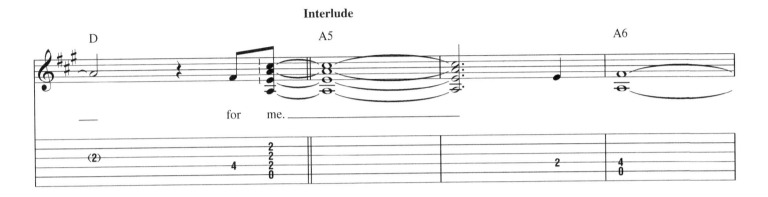

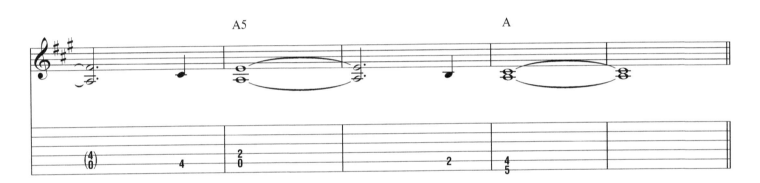

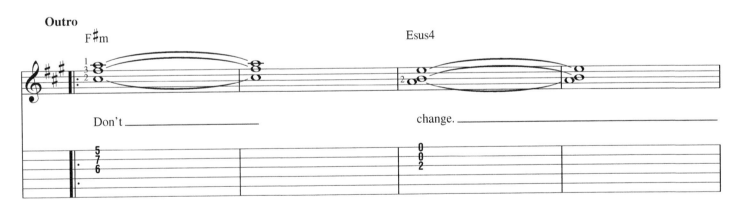

867-5309/Jenny

Words and Music by Alex Call and James Keller

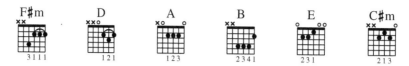

Strum Pattern: 4, 6
Pick Pattern: 5, 6

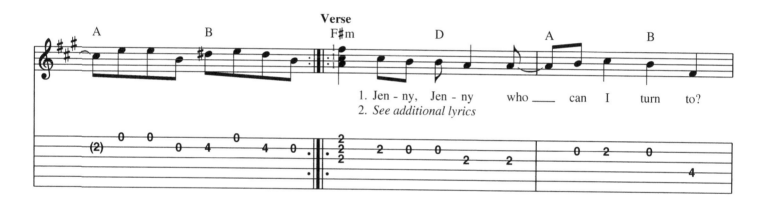

1. Jen - ny, Jen - ny who ___ can I turn to?
2. *See additional lyrics*

You give me some-thing I ____ can hold on to.

I know you'll think I'm like the oth-ers be - fore,

Copyright © 1981 by Unichappell Music Inc., Warner-Tamerlane Publishing Corp., Mt. Krakatau Music and Elisha James Music
All Rights for Mt. Krakatau Music Controlled and Administered by Warner-Tamerlane Publishing Corp.
International Copyright Secured   All Rights Reserved

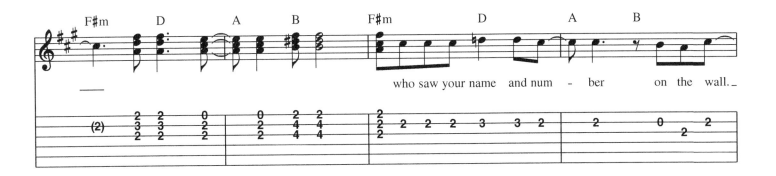

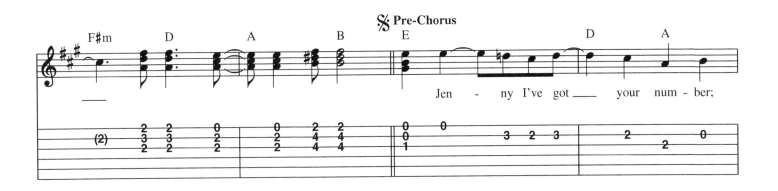

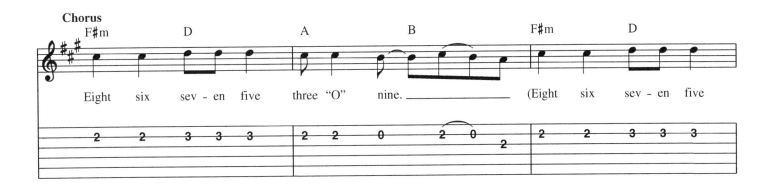

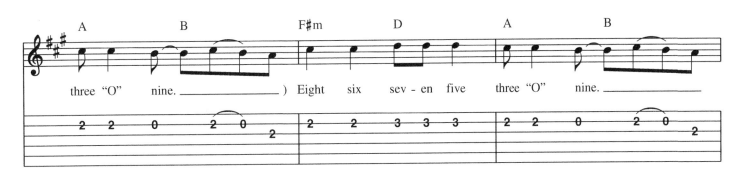

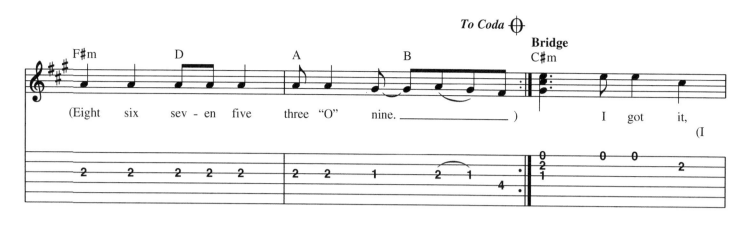

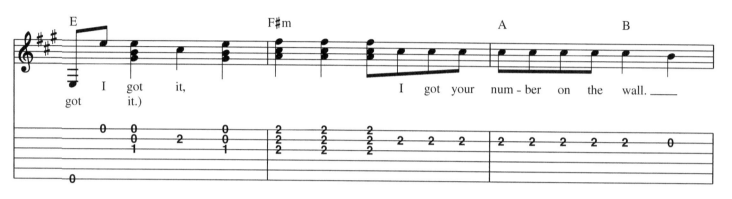

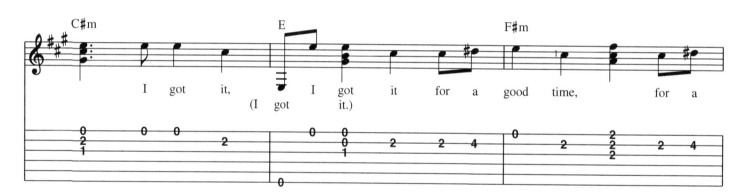

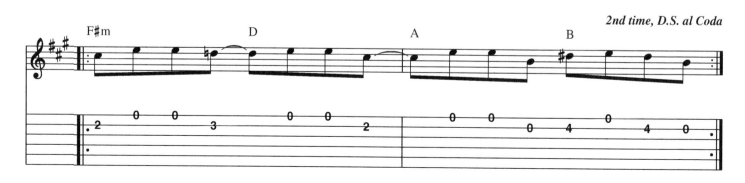

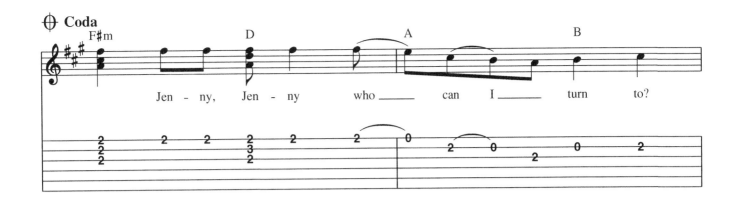

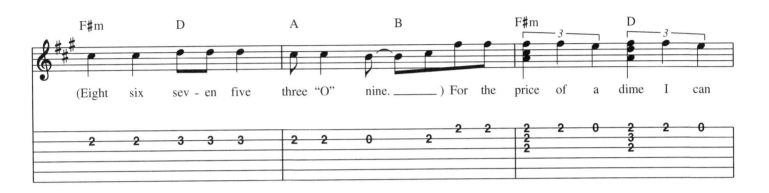

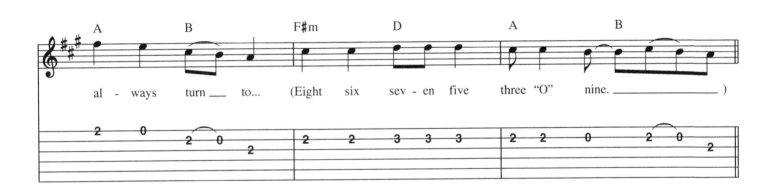

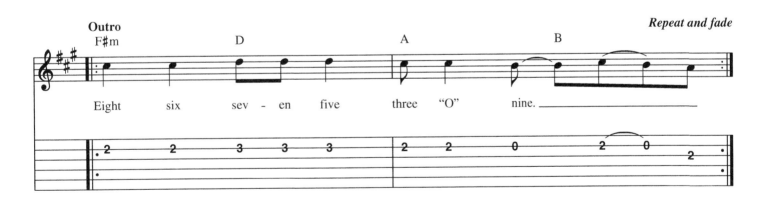

Additional Lyrics

2. Jenny, Jenny you're the girl for me.
You don't know me but you make me so happy.
I tried to call you before
But I lost my nerve.
I tried my imagination
But I was disturbed.

Every Breath You Take

Music and Lyrics by Sting

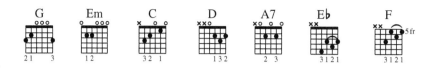

Strum Pattern: 4
Pick Pattern: 3

© 1983 G.M. SUMNER
Administered by EMI MUSIC PUBLISHING LIMITED
All Rights Reserved   International Copyright Secured   Used by Permission

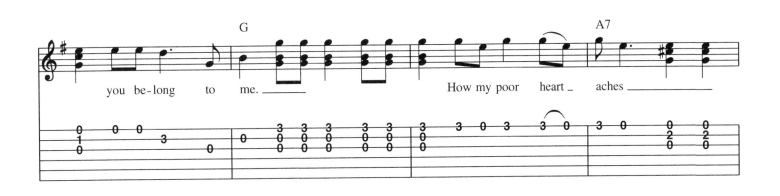

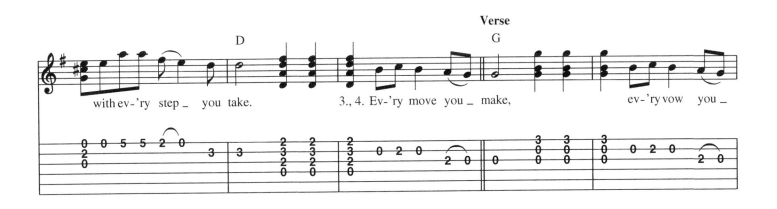

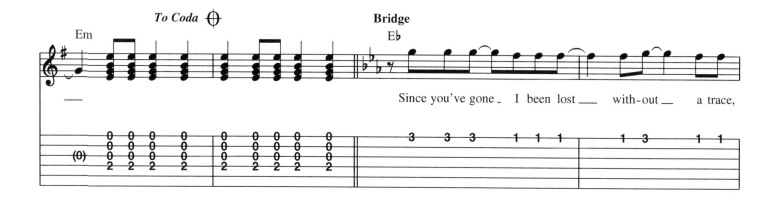

Since you've gone _ I been lost _ with-out _ a trace,

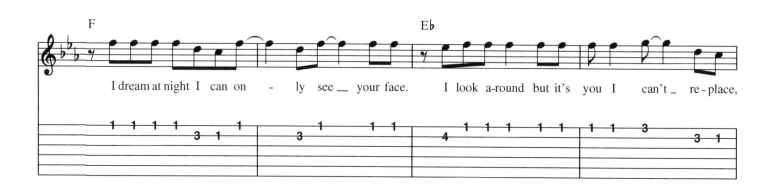

I dream at night I can on - ly see _ your face. I look a-round but it's you I can't _ re-place,

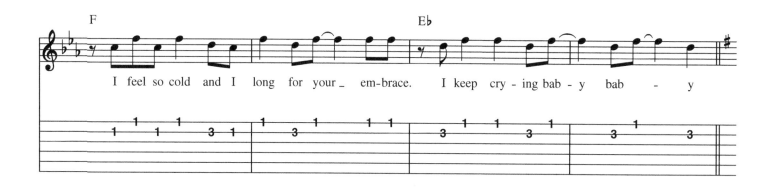

I feel so cold and I long for your _ em-brace. I keep cry - ing bab - y bab - y

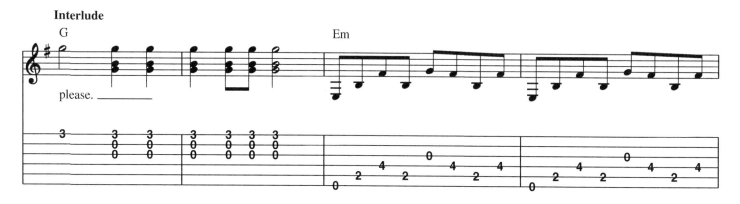

please. _____

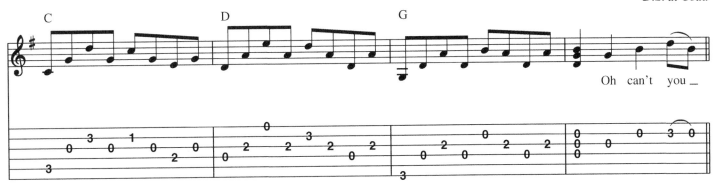

Oh can't you _

Coda

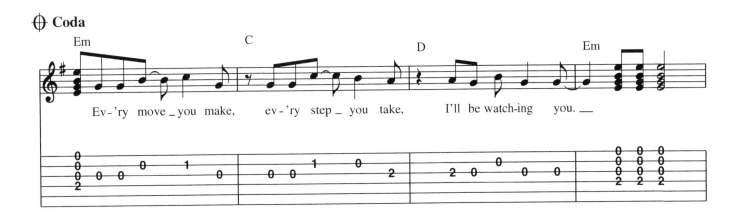

Ev-'ry move _ you make, ev-'ry step _ you take, I'll be watch-ing you. _

I'll be watch-ing you. _____

Additional Lyrics

2. Ev'ry single day, ev'ry word you say,
   Ev'ry game you play, ev'ry night you stay,
   I'll be watching you.

Fight for Your Right (To Party)

Words and Music by Rick Rubin, Adam Horovitz and Adam Yauch

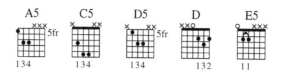

*Tune down 1/2 step:
(low to high) Eb-Ab-Db-Gb-Bb-Eb

Strum Pattern: 5

Intro
Moderately

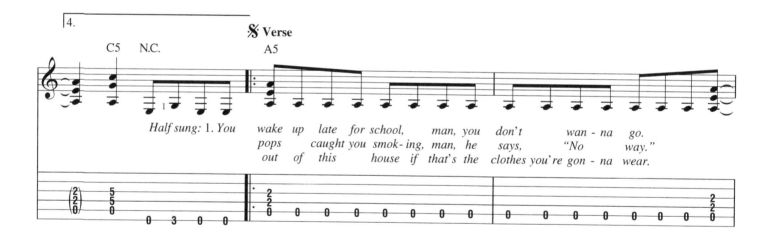

*Optional: To match recording, tune down 1/2 step.

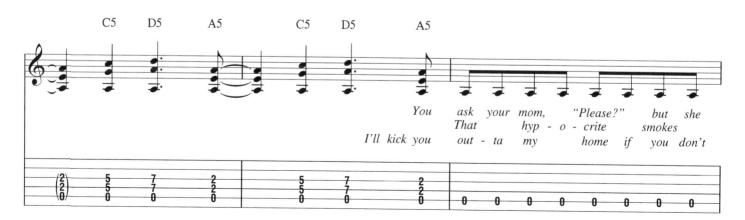

Copyright © 1986 American Def Tunes, Inc., Universal - PolyGram International Publishing, Inc. and Brooklyn Dust Music
All Rights on behalf of American Def Tunes, Inc. Administered by Sony/ATV Music Publishing LLC, 8 Music Square West, Nashville, TN 37203
All Rights on behalf of Brooklyn Dust Music Controlled and Administered by Universal - PolyGram International Publishing, Inc.
International Copyright Secured   All Rights Reserved

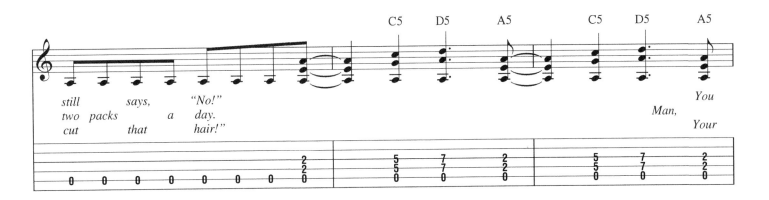

still   says,   "No!"
two packs   a   day.
cut   that   hair!"
                                                                          You
                                                             Man,
                                                             Your

missed   two   class - es   and   no   home - work,
liv - in'   at   home   is   such   a   drag.
mom   bust - ed   in   and   said,   "What's   that   noise?"

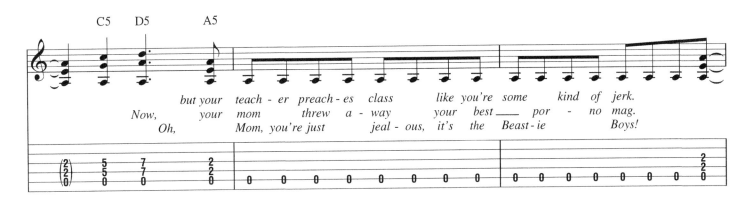

but your   teach - er preach - es   class   like you're some   kind of   jerk.
Now,   your   mom   threw   a - way   your   best ___ por - no mag.
Oh,   Mom, you're just   jeal - ous,   it's   the   Beast - ie   Boys!

𝄋 𝄋 **Chorus**

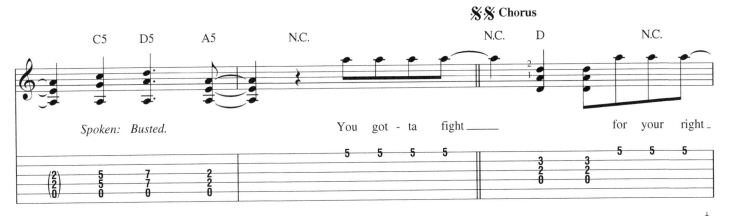

Spoken: Busted.   You   got - ta   fight ___   for   your   right ___

To Coda 1 𝄌

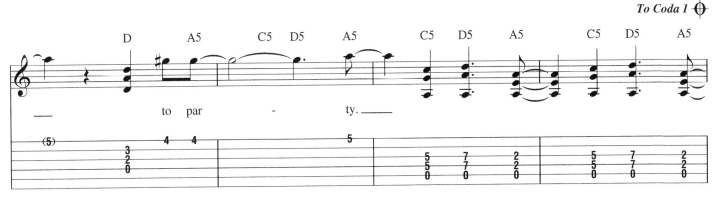

___   to   par   -   ty. ___

Free Fallin'

Words and Music by Tom Petty and Jeff Lynne

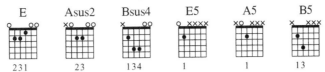

Strum Pattern: 6
Pick Pattern: 6

Intro
Moderate Rock

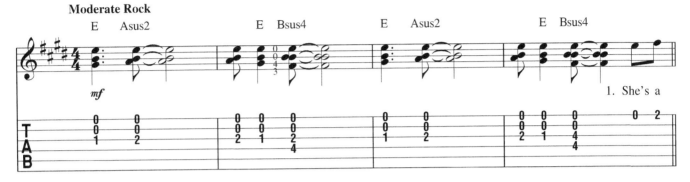

1. She's a

Verse

good girl, ___ loves her ma - ma, loves Je - sus, ___ and A -

mer - i - ca, too. ___ She's a good girl, ___ cra - zy 'bout El - vis, loves

hor - ses, ___ and her boy - friend, too. ___

Copyright © 1989 Gone Gator Music and EMI April Music Inc.
All Rights Reserved   Used by Permission

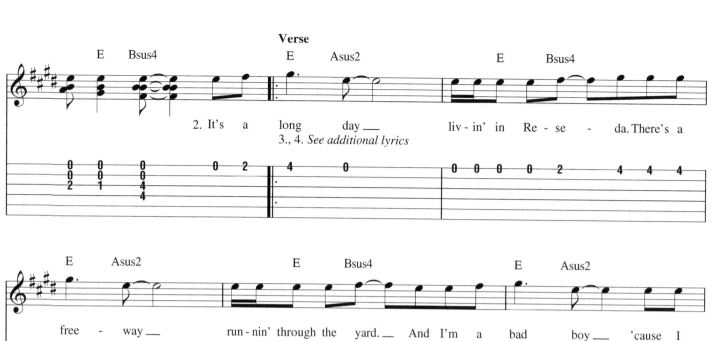

Verse

2. It's a long day ___ liv-in' in Re-se - da. There's a

3., 4. *See additional lyrics*

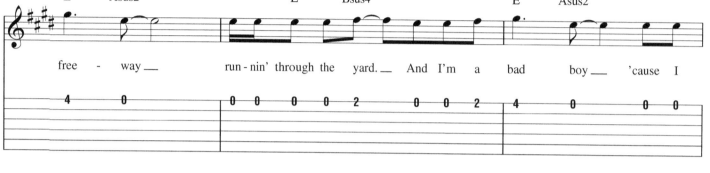

free - way ___ run-nin' through the yard. ___ And I'm a bad boy ___ 'cause I

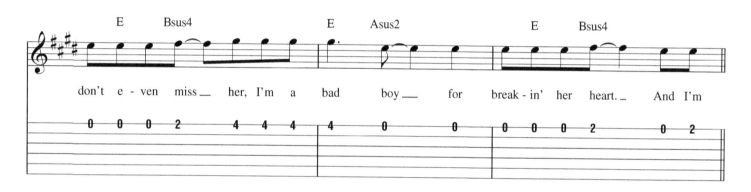

don't e - ven miss ___ her, I'm a bad boy ___ for break-in' her heart. ___ And I'm

Chorus

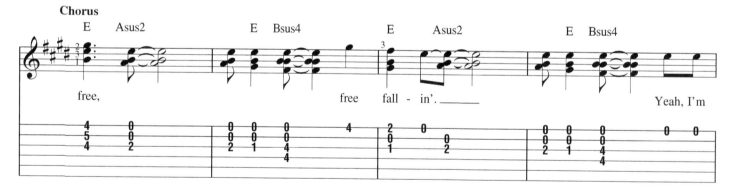

free,   free fall - in'. ___   Yeah, I'm

free,   free fall - in'. ___   3. All the

Interlude

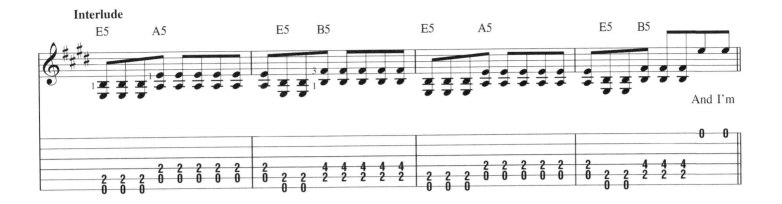

And I'm

Outro-Chorus

free,   free   fall - in'._____   Yeah, I'm

Repeat and fade

free,   free   fall - in'._____   And I'm

Additional Lyrics

3. All the vampires walkin' through the valley
   Move west down Ventura Boulevard.
   And all the bad boys are standing in the shadows.
   And the good girls are home with broken hearts.

4. Wanna glide down over Mulholland.
   I wanna write her name in the sky.
   I wanna free fall out into nothin'.
   Gonna leave this world for a while.

Heart and Soul

Words and Music by Mike Chapman and Nicky Chinn

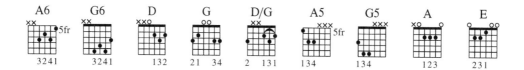

Strum Pattern: 3, 5
Pick Pattern: 1, 4

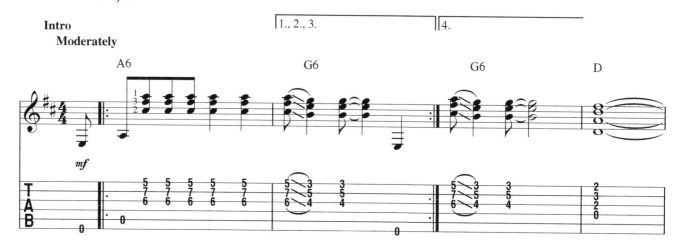

1. Two o' clock this morn - ing, _____
2. Can't you see her stand - ing there?

if she should come a - call - ing, I would - n't dream of turn -
See how she looks, see how _____ she cares. I let her steal the night

Copyright © 1981 by Universal Music - MGB Songs
International Copyright Secured All Rights Reserved

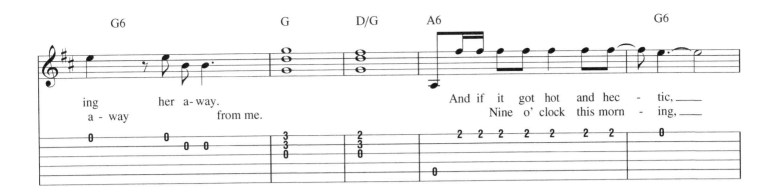

Chorus

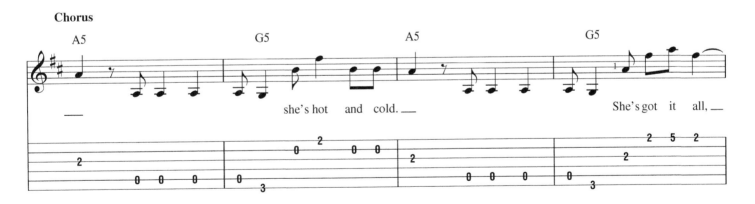

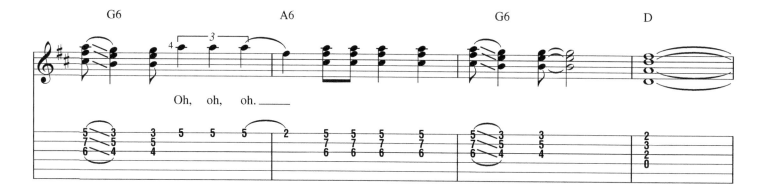

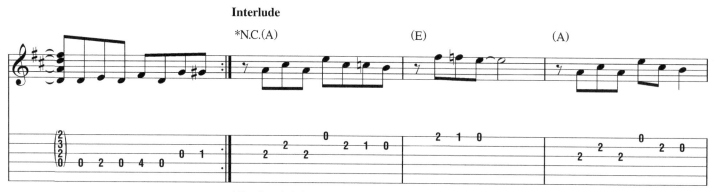

*Chord symbols in parentheses reflect implied harmony.

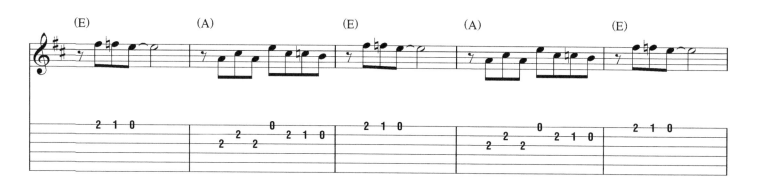

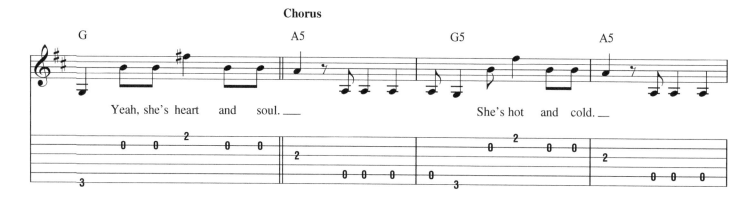

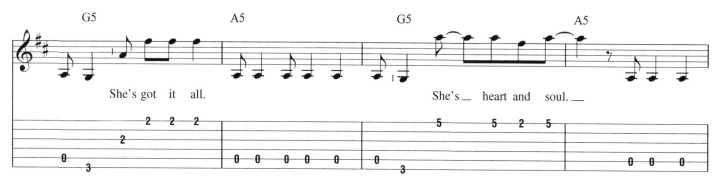

Heartbreaker

Words and Music by Cliff Wade and Geoff Gill

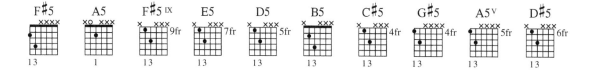

*Tune down 1/2 step:
(low to high) Eb-Ab-Db-Gb-Bb-Eb

Strum Pattern: 1

Intro

Moderately fast

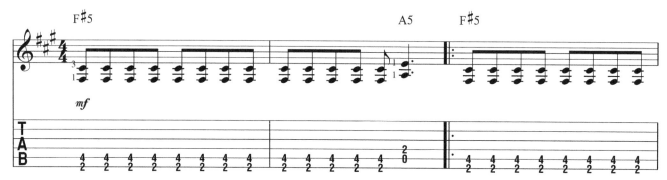

*Optional: To match recording, tune down 1/2 step.

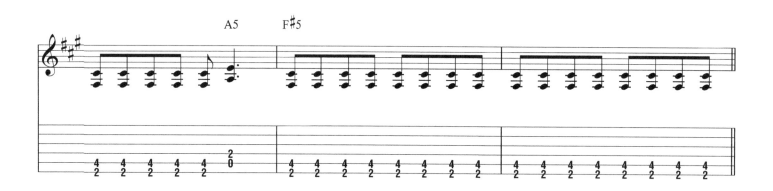

Verse

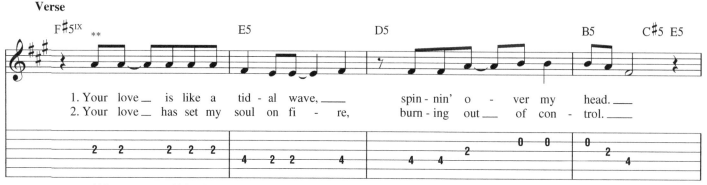

1. Your love __ is like a tid-al wave, ___ spin-nin' o-ver my head. __
2. Your love __ has set my soul on fi-re, burn-ing out __ of con-trol. __

**Sung one octave higher throughout.

Copyright © 1978, 1980 GGA LIMITED and UNIVERSAL/DICK JAMES MUSIC LIMITED
All Rights for the United States and Canada Controlled and Administered by UNIVERSAL - SONGS OF POLYGRAM INTERNATIONAL, INC.
All Rights Reserved   Used by Permission

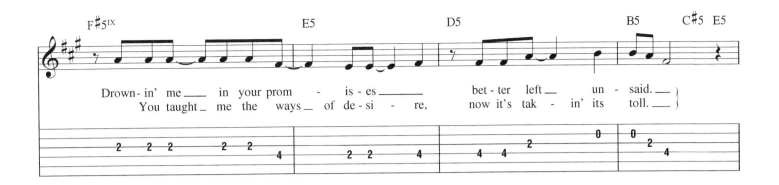

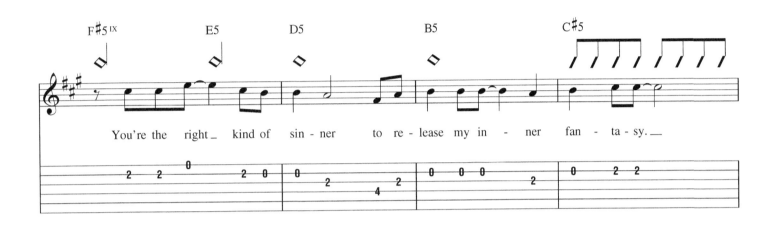

Chorus

Bridge

You're the right __ kind of sin - ner to re - lease my in - ner fan-ta - sy. __

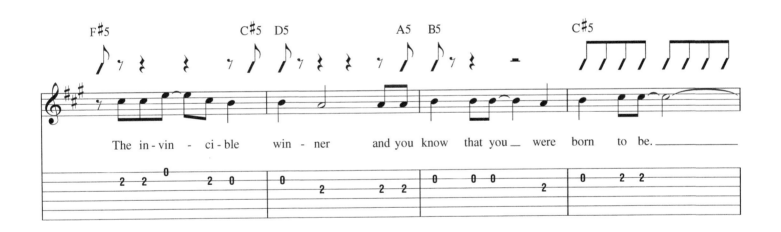

The in - vin - ci - ble win - ner and you know that you __ were born to be. _____

Chorus

You're a heart - break - er, dream - mak - er, love - tak - er, don't you

Here I Go Again

Words and Music by Bernie Marsden and David Coverdale

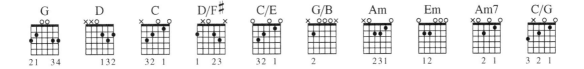

Strum Pattern: 4
Pick Pattern: 5

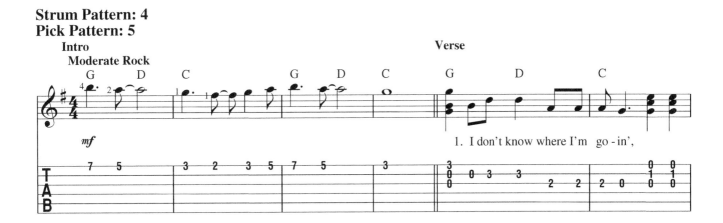

© 1982 EMI MUSIC PUBLISHING LTD. and WB MUSIC CORP.
All Rights for EMI MUSIC PUBLISHING LTD. in the U.S. and Canada
Controlled and Administered by EMI LONGITUDE MUSIC
All Rights Reserved   International Copyright Secured   Used by Permission

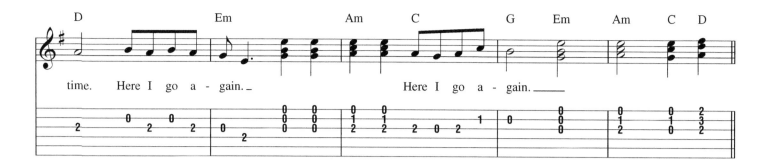

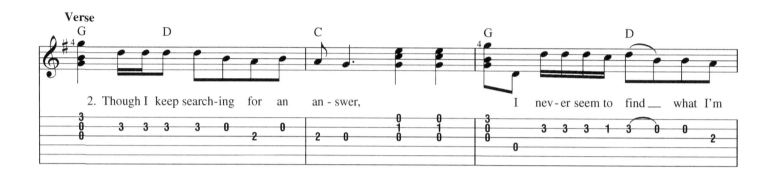

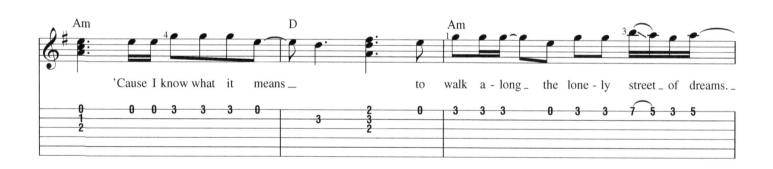

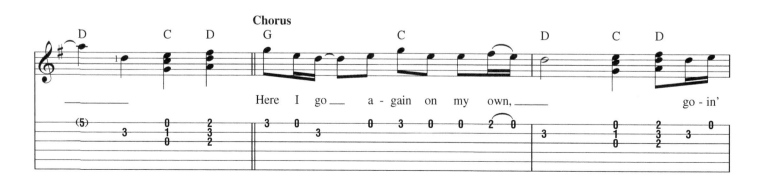

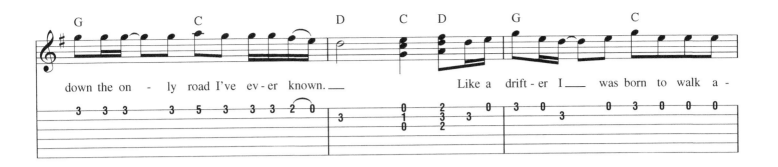

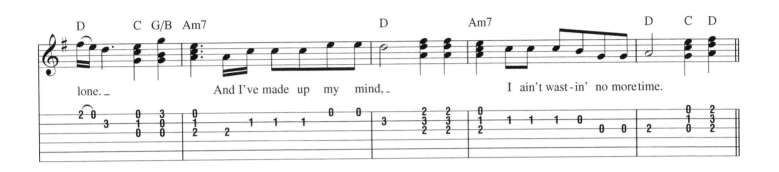

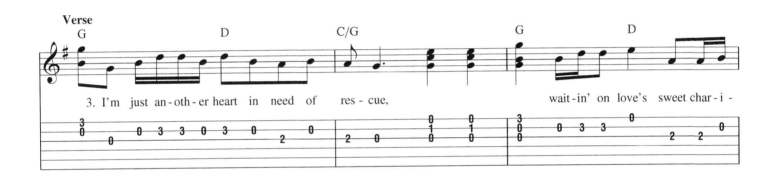

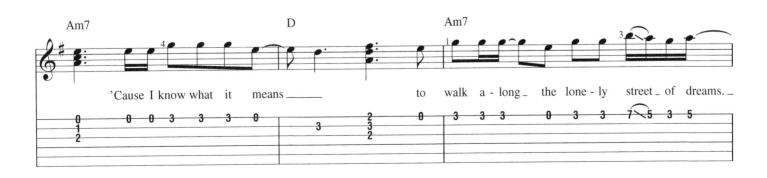

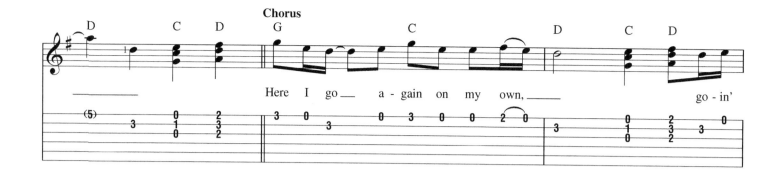

Here I go ___ a - gain on my own, ____ go - in'

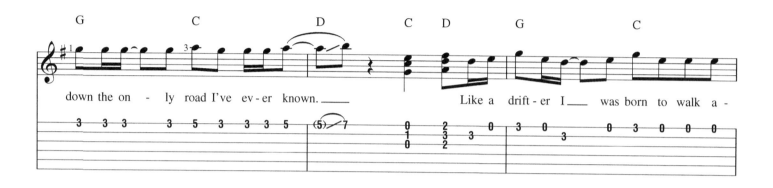

down the on - ly road I've ev - er known. ____ Like a drift - er I ___ was born to walk a -

lone. ___ And I've made up my mind, ____ I ain't wast - in' no more

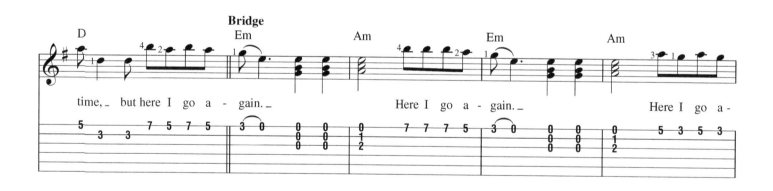

time, _ but here I go a - gain. _ Here I go a - gain. _ Here I go a -

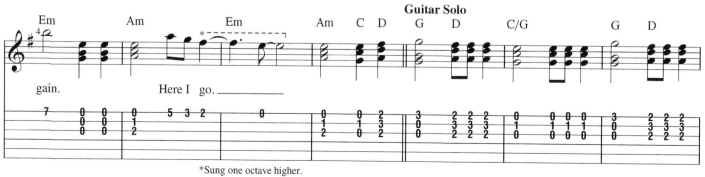

gain. Here I go. ___

*Sung one octave higher.

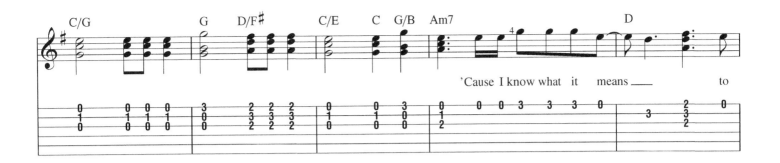

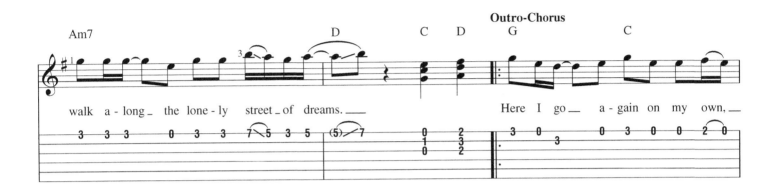

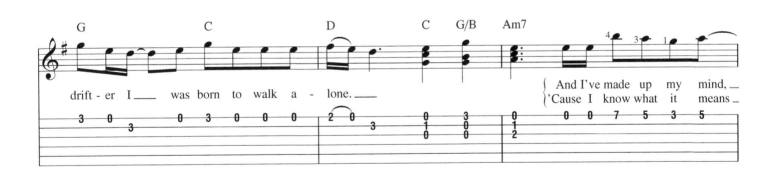

Heaven's on Fire

Words and Music by Paul Stanley and Desmond Child

Copyright © 1984 HORI PRODUCTIONS AMERICA, INC. and DESMOBILE MUSIC CO., INC.
All Rights Controlled and Administered by UNIVERSAL - POLYGRAM INTERNATIONAL PUBLISHING, INC.
All Rights Reserved   Used by Permission

You know the way to give me what I need.
You drive me cra-zy when you start to tease.
Just let me love you and you'll
And you can bring the de - vil

Chorus

ne - ver leave.
to his knees.
Feel my heat tak - ing you high - er.

Burn with me. Heav - en's on fire. Paint the sky

2nd time, D.S. al Fine
Fine

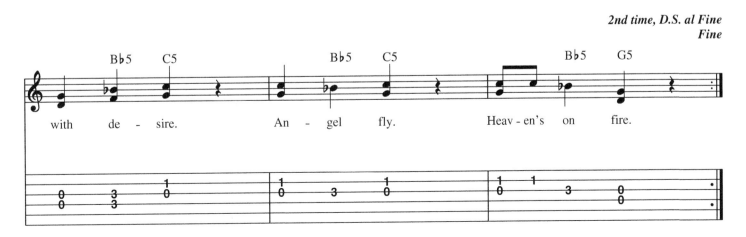

with de - sire. An - gel fly. Heav - en's on fire.

Hold on Loosely

Words and Music by Jeff Carlisi, Don Barnes and Jim Peterik

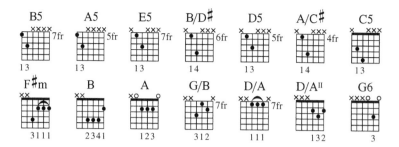

Strum Pattern: 1, 6

Intro
Moderate Rock

𝄋 Verse

1., 3. You see it all a - round you, ___
2. It's so damn eas - y,

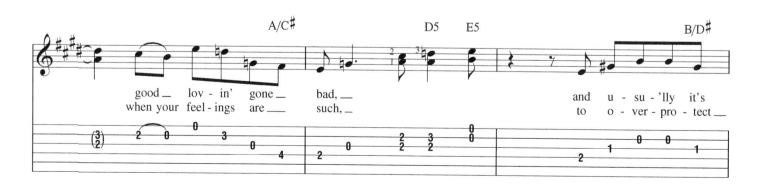

good __ lov - in' gone __ bad, ___ and u - su - 'lly it's
when your feel - ings are ___ such, ___ to o - ver - pro - tect ___

Copyright © 1981 by Universal Music - MGB Songs, WB Music Corp. and Easy Action Music
All Rights for Easy Action Music Administered by WB Music Corp.
International Copyright Secured   All Rights Reserved

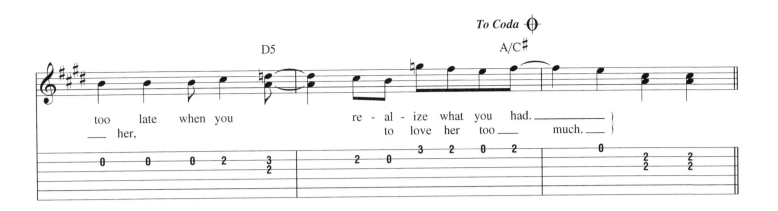

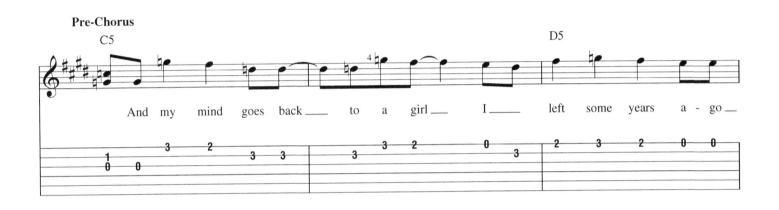

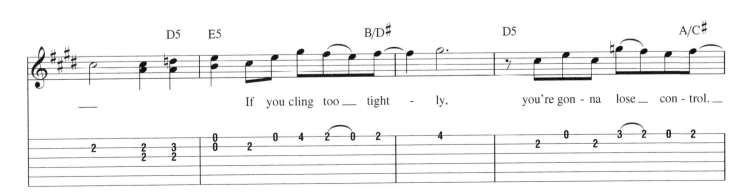

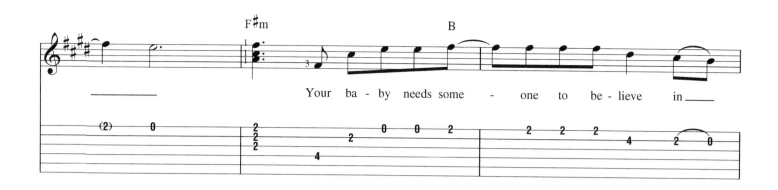

Your ba - by needs some - one to be - lieve in _____

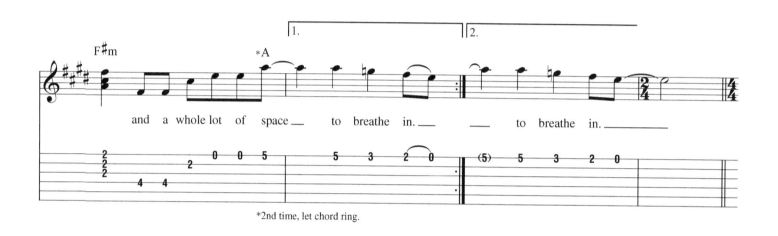

and a whole lot of space ____ to breathe in. ____ ____ to breathe in. _____

*2nd time, let chord ring.

Bridge

Don't let her slip a - way.

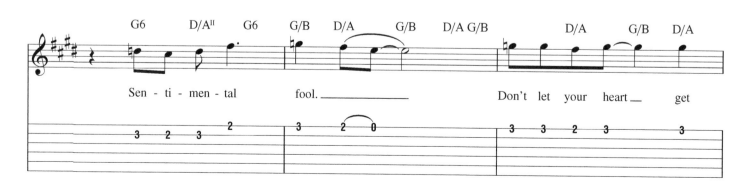

Sen - ti - men - tal fool. _____ Don't let your heart ____ get

Chorus

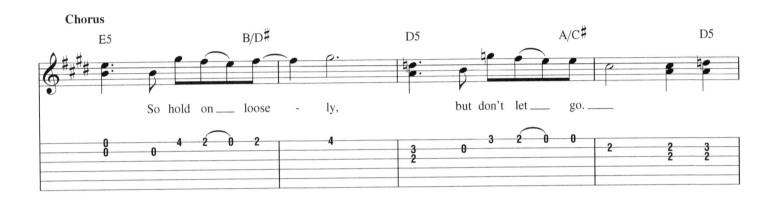

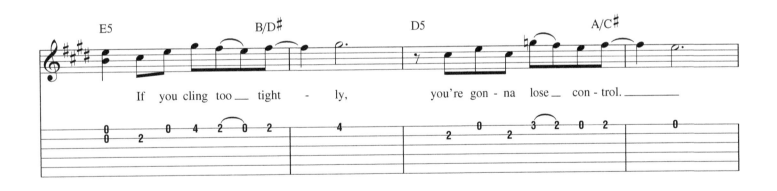

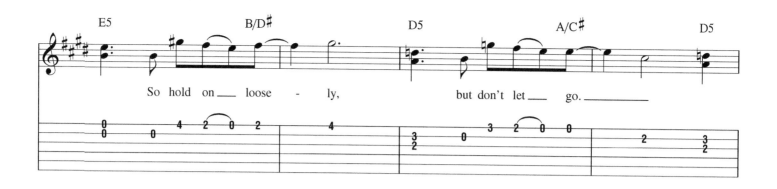

So hold on __ loose - ly, but don't let __ go. __

If you cling too __ tight - ly, you're gon-na lose __ it. you're gon - na lose con - trol. __

Outro-Guitar Solo
w/ Voc. ad lib.

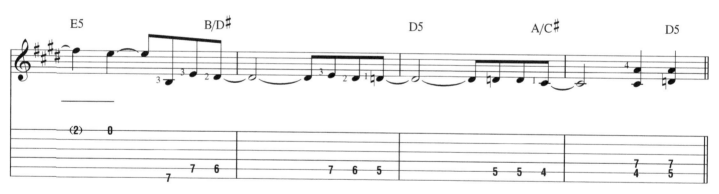

Repeat and fade

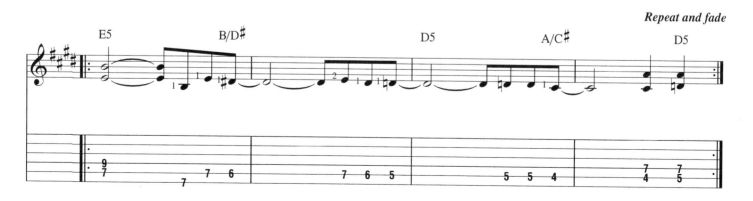

Jessie's Girl

Words and Music by Rick Springfield

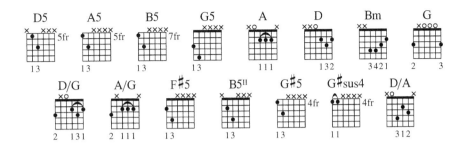

Strum Pattern: 1
Pick Pattern: 2

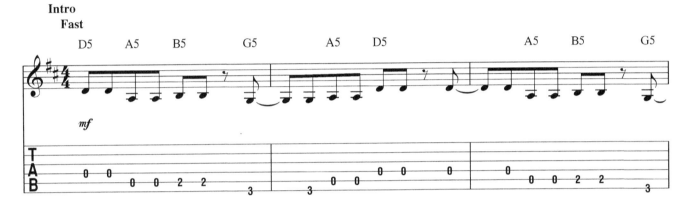

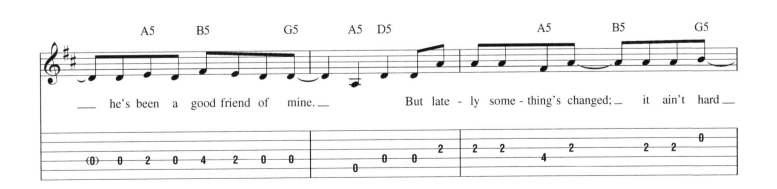

Copyright © 1981 UNIVERSAL - SONGS OF POLYGRAM INTERNATIONAL, INC.
All Rights Reserved   Used by Permission

Pre-Chorus

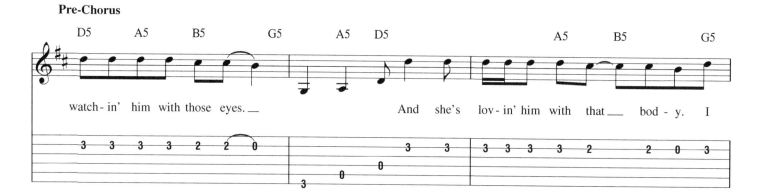

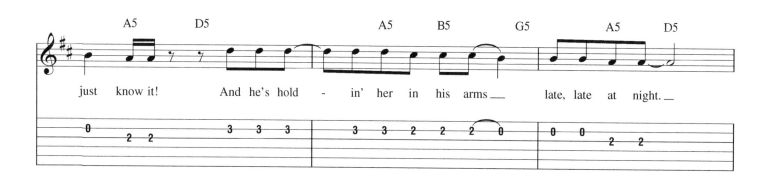

Chorus

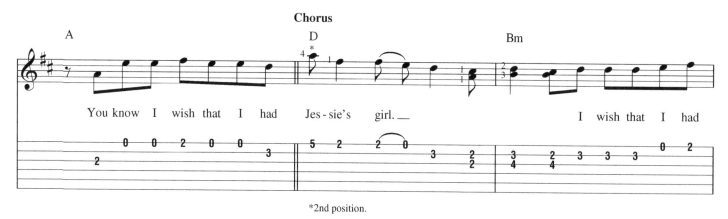

*2nd position.

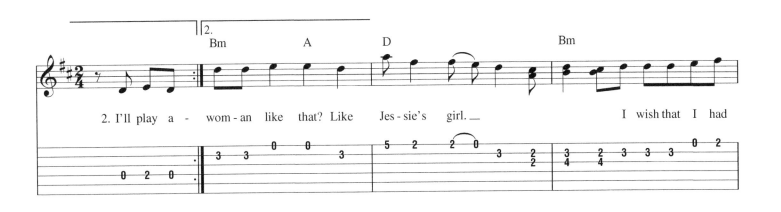

2. I'll play a - wom - an like that? Like Jes - sie's girl. ___ I wish that I had

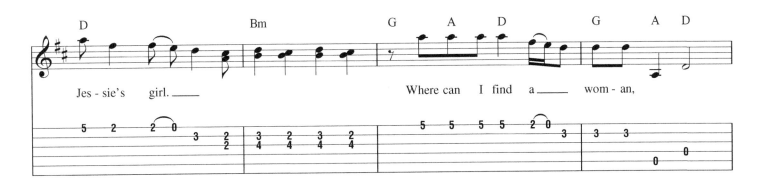

Jes - sie's girl. ___ Where can I find a ___ wom - an,

Bridge

where can I find a ___ wom - an like that?

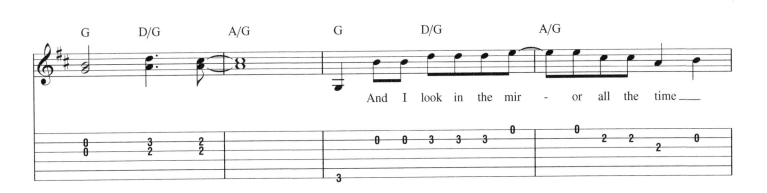

And I look in the mir - or all the time ___

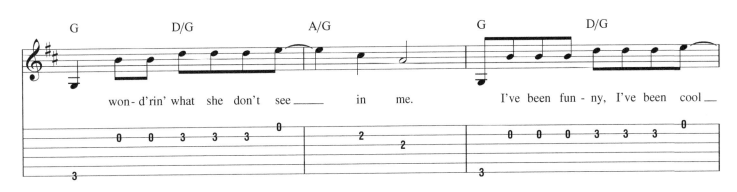

won - d'rin' what she don't see ___ in me. I've been fun - ny, I've been cool ___

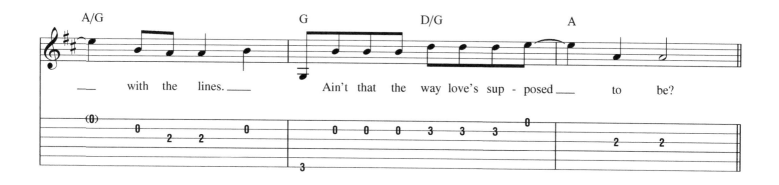

with the lines. ___ Ain't that the way love's sup - posed ___ to *be?

Interlude

Tell me

where can I find a _____ wom - an like that?

Guitar Solo

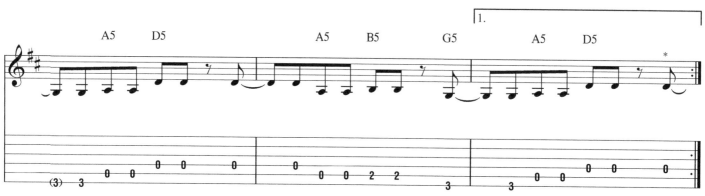

*Tie into beat 1 on repeat.

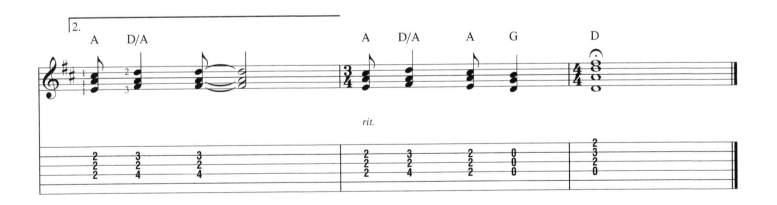

Additional Lyrics

2. I'll play along with this charade.
   There doesn't seem to be a reason to change.
   You know, I feel so dirty when they start talkin' cute.
   I wanna tell her that I love her, but the point is prob'ly moot.

I Love Rock 'n Roll

Words and Music by Alan Merrill and Jake Hooker

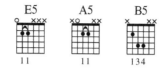

*Strum Pattern: 1, 5

Intro

Moderately slow rock, in 2

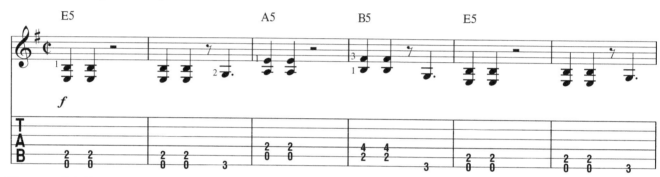

*Use pattern 10 for $\frac{2}{4}$ meas.

Verse

saw him danc - ing there ___ by the re - cord ma - chine.
2. *See additional lyrics*
3. *Instrumental*

Copyright © 1975, 1982 Rak Publishing Ltd. for the World
Copyright Renewed 2003
All Rights for the U.S.A. and Canada Controlled by Finchley Music Corp.
Administered by Music & Media International, Inc.
International Copyright Secured   All Rights Reserved

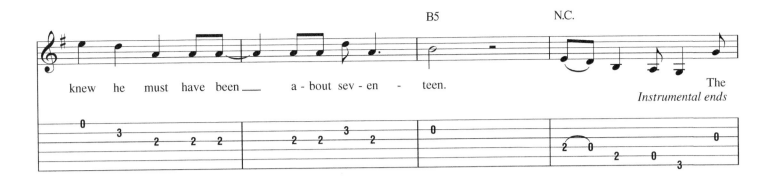

knew he must have been __ a - bout sev - en - teen. The
Instrumental ends

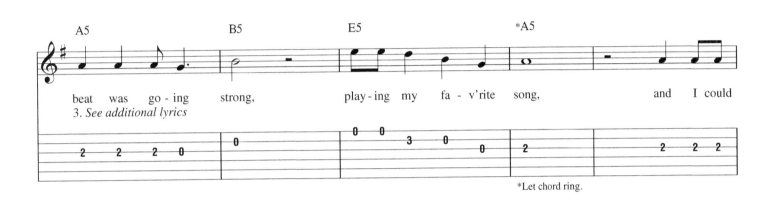

beat was go - ing strong, play - ing my fa - v'rite song, and I could
3. *See additional lyrics*

*Let chord ring.

tell it would - n't be long 'til he was with me, yeah, me. And I could

tell it would - n't be long 'til he was with me, yeah, me, sing - in'

**Third time, chords tacet.

Chorus
w/ Intro pattern

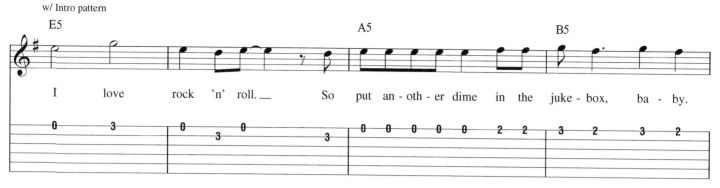

I love rock 'n' roll. __ So put an-oth-er dime in the juke-box, ba - by.

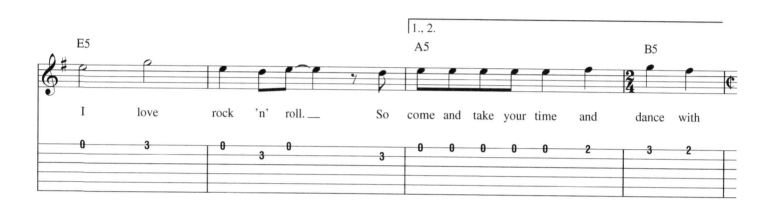

I love rock 'n' roll. __ So come and take your time and dance with

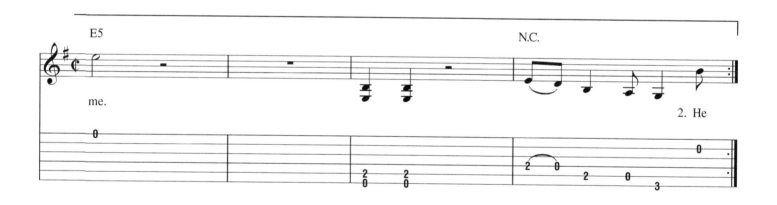

me. 2. He

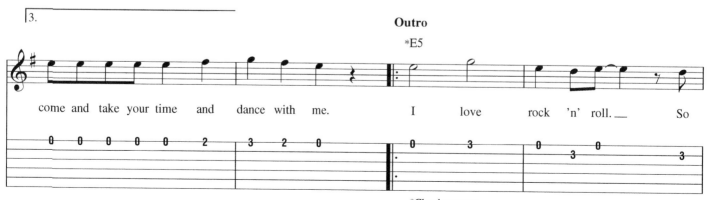

come and take your time and dance with me. I love rock 'n' roll. __ So

*Chords resume.

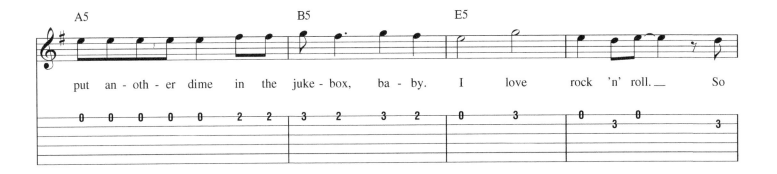

put an-oth-er dime in the juke-box, ba-by. I love rock 'n' roll. __ So

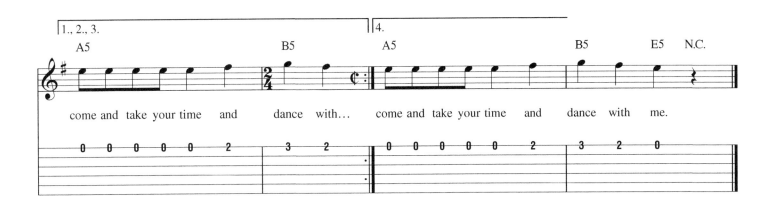

1., 2., 3.

come and take your time and dance with...

4.

come and take your time and dance with me.

Additional Lyrics

2. He smiled, so I got up and asked for his name.
   "That don't matter," he said, "'cause it's all the same."
   I said, "Can I take you home
   Where we can be alone?"
   And next we were moving on
   And he was with me, yeah, me.
   And next we were moving on.
   And he was with me, yeah, me, singin'…

3. *Instrumental*
   I said, "Can I take you home
   Where we can be alone?"
   And next we were moving on
   And he was with me, yeah, me.
   And we'll be movin' on and singin' that same old song,
   Yeah with me, singin'…

Jack and Diane

Words and Music by John Mellencamp

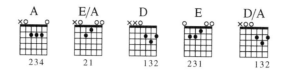

Strum Pattern: 2, 6
Pick Pattern: 2, 6

Intro
Moderately

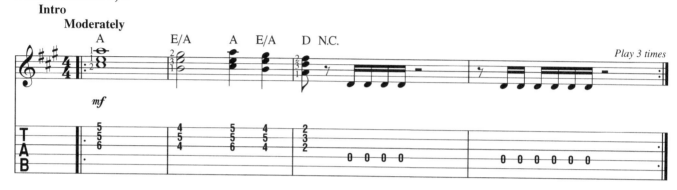

Play 3 times

Verse

1. Lit-tle dit-ty 'bout Jack and Di - ane, _____ *Spoken: two American kids growin' up in the heartland.*

Lyrics in italics are spoken throughout.

Jack-ie gon-na be _ a foot-ball star. _____ *Diane's the debutante back seat of Jackie's car.*

Interlude

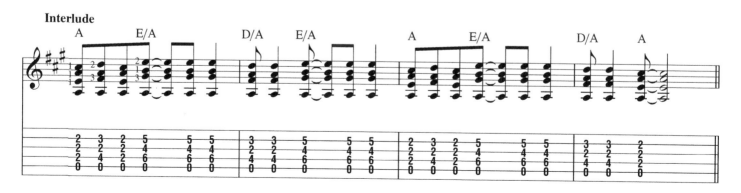

© 1982 EMI FULL KEEL MUSIC
All Rights Reserved   International Copyright Secured   Used by Permission

2. Suck-in' on a chil-i dog   out-side the Tast-ee-Freez, _____   *Diane sittin' on Jackie's lap, he's*
3. *See additional lyrics*

got his hands between her knees.   Jack-ie say, "Hey, Di-ane, let's run off be-hind the shad-y   trees. _____

Chorus

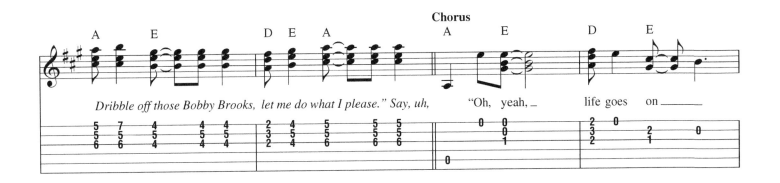

Dribble off those Bobby Brooks, let me do what I please." Say, uh,   "Oh, yeah, _   life goes   on _____

long af-ter the thrill   of liv-in' is _ gone." _{ *They say, uh,*   "Oh, yeah, _   life goes   on, _____
                                                         Oh, yeah, _ they say, "life goes   on, _____

To Coda

Interlude

long af-ter the thrill   of liv-in' is _ gone." _ *They walk on.*

Coda

2nd time, D.S. al Coda

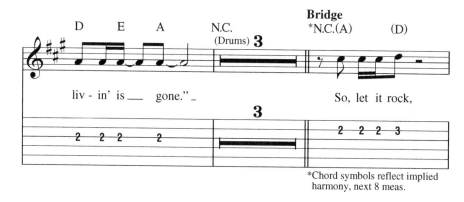

*Chord symbols reflect implied
harmony, next 8 meas.

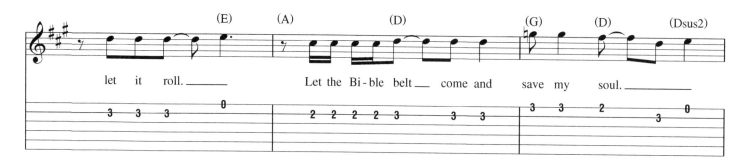

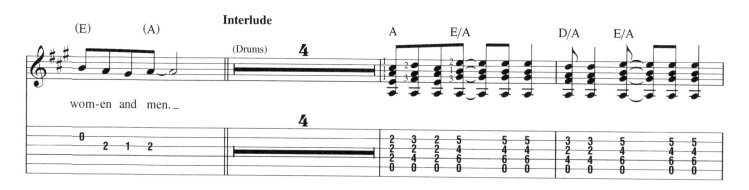

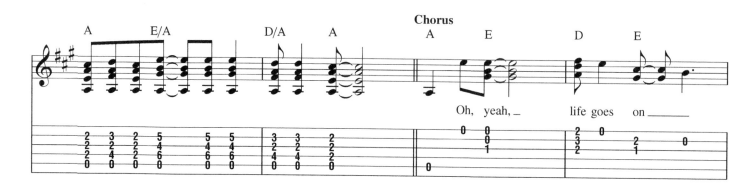

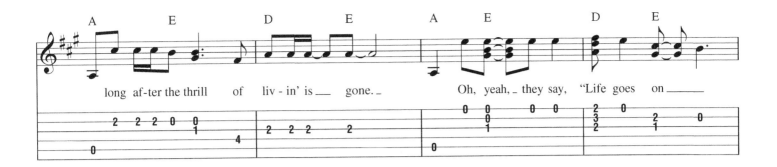

long af-ter the thrill of liv-in' is __ gone. __ Oh, yeah, _ they say, "Life goes on _____

Outro

long af-ter the thrill of liv-in' is __ gone." _ A lit-tle dit-ty 'bout

Jack and Di-ane, _____ *two American kids doin' the best they can.*

Repeat and fade

Additional Lyrics

3. Jackie sits back, collects his thoughts for a moment,
   Scratches his head and does his best James Dean.
   "Well, then there Diane, we oughta run off to the city."
   Diane says, "Baby, you ain't missin' nothing."
   But Jackie say, ah,

Just Like Heaven

Words and Music by Robert Smith, Laurence Tolhurst, Simon Gallup, Paul S. Thompson and Boris Williams

Copyright © 1987 by Fiction Songs Ltd.
All Rights for the World Administered by Universal MGB Music Publishing Ltd.
All Rights for the U.S. Administered by Universal Music - MGB Songs
International Copyright Secured   All Rights Reserved

twist-ing in ___ the wa - ter, you're just like a dream. ___

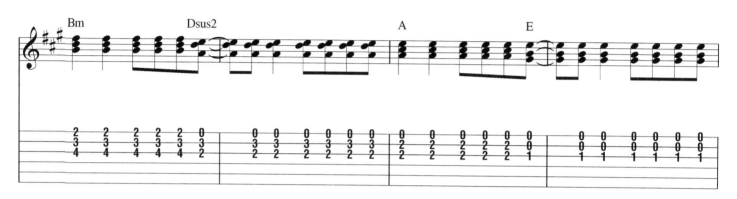

D.S. al Coda

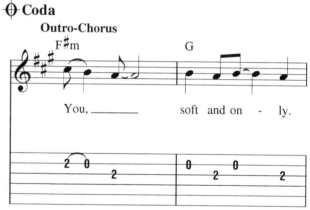

You, _____ soft and on - ly.

You, _____ lost and lone - ly. You _____ are just like heav-en.

Additional Lyrics

2. Spinning on that dizzy edge,
   I kissed her face and kissed her head,
   And dreamed of all the diff'rent ways
   I had to make her grow.
   "Why are you so far away?"
   She said, "Why won't you ever know that
   I'm in love with you?
   I am in love with you."

3. Daylight licked me into shape.
   I must have been asleep for days.
   And moving lips to breathe her name,
   I opened up my eyes.
   Found myself alone, alone, alone,
   Above the raging sea
   That stole the only girl I loved,
   And drowned her deep inside of me.

Like a Rock

Words and Music by Bob Seger

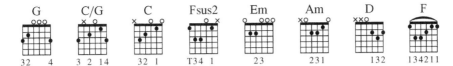

*Capo I

Strum Pattern: 6
Pick Pattern: 4

*Optional: To match recording, place capo at 1st fret.

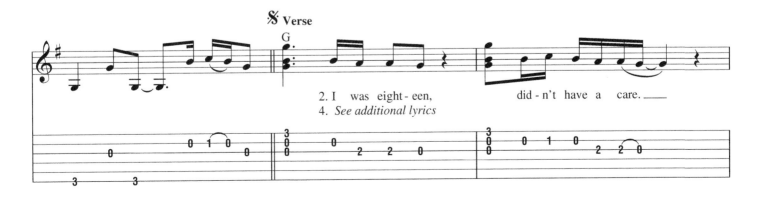

Copyright © 1985, 1986 Gear Publishing Co.
All Rights Reserved   Used by Permission

Work - in' for pea - nuts, not a dime __ to spare. __ But I was lean and

sol - id ev -'ry - where, __ like a rock.

Verse

3. My hands were stead- y, my eyes were clear and bright. __ My walk had pur - pose, my
5. *See additional lyrics*

To Coda ⊕

steps were quick and light, ___ and I held firm - ly to what I felt __ was right, __ like a

Chorus

rock. Like a rock, I was

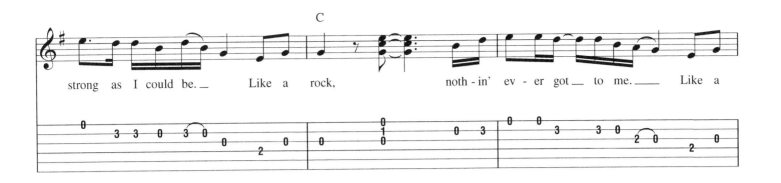

strong as I could be._ Like a rock, noth-in' ev-er got_ to me.__ Like a

rock, I was some-thing to see,_____ like a rock.

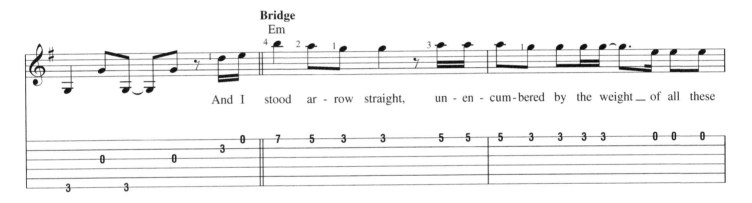

Bridge

And I stood ar-row straight, un-en-cum-bered by the weight_ of all these

hus-tlers and their schemes._ I stood proud, I stood tall,___

high_ a-bove it all.__ I still_ be-lieved_ in my dreams._

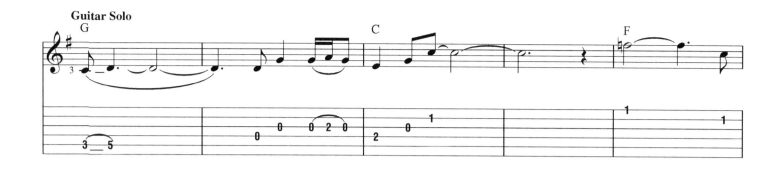

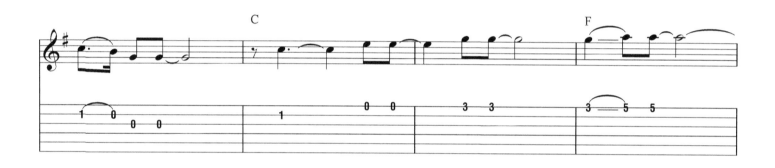

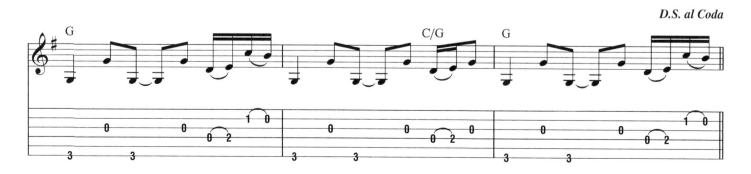

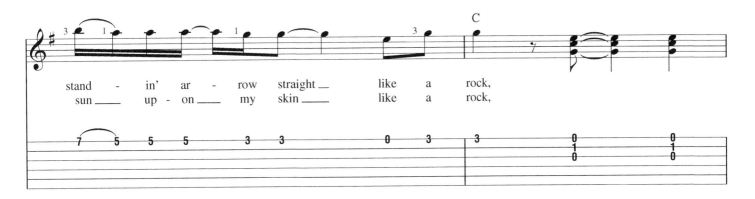

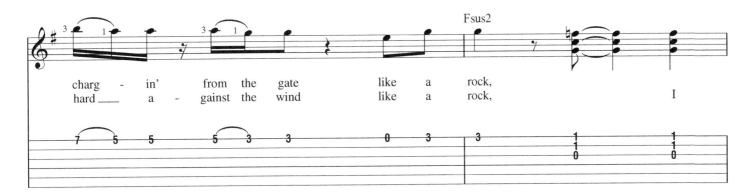

Additional Lyrics

4. Twenty years now; where'd they go?
   Twenty years, I don't know.
   I sit and I wonder sometimes
   Where they've gone.

5. And sometimes late at night,
   When I'm bathed in the firelight.
   The moon comes callin' a ghostly white,
   And I recall, I recall.

Money for Nothing

Words and Music by Mark Knopfler and Sting

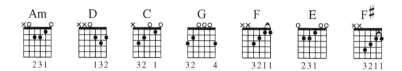

*Tune down 1 step:
(low to high) D-G-C-F-A-D

Strum Pattern: 2
Pick Pattern: 4

Intro
Moderate Rock

*Optional: To match recording, tune down 1 step.
**First time, chords tacet.

𝄋 **Verse**

1. Look at them __ yo - yos. That's __ the way to do it. __ Play the gui - tar on the
4. *See additional lyrics*

Copyright © 1985 Straitjacket Songs Limited and G.M. Sumner
G.M. Sumner Administered by EMI Music Publishing Ltd.
International Copyright Secured   All Rights Reserved

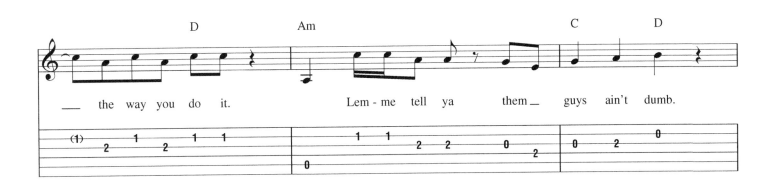

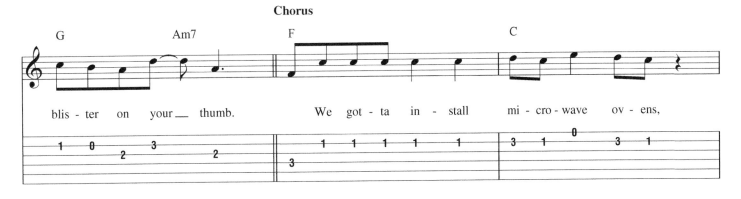

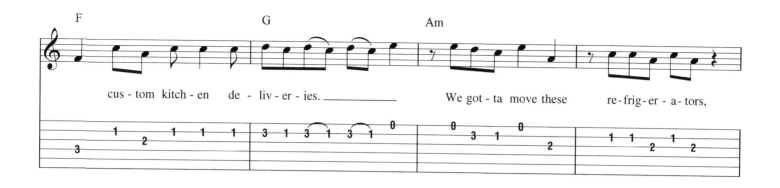

cus - tom kitch - en   de - liv - er - ies. _____   We got - ta move these   re - frig - er - a - tors,

we got - ta move these   col - or T V's. _____

Interlude

To Coda ⊕

Chorus

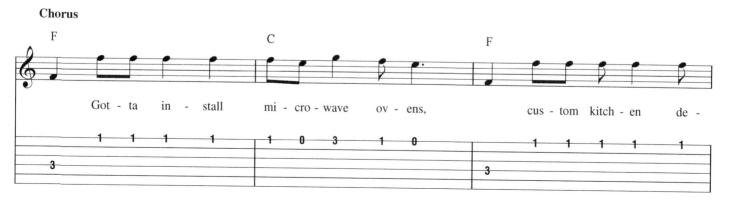

Got - ta in - stall   mi - cro - wave   ov - ens,   cus - tom kitch - en   de -

liv - er - ies._____ We got - ta move these re - frig - er - a - tors,

D.S. al Coda
(no repeat)

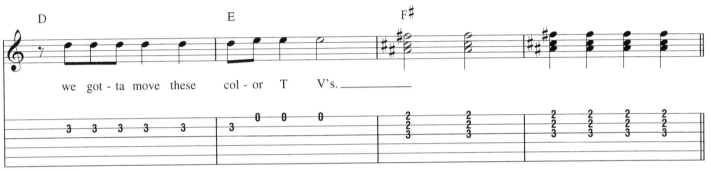

we got - ta move these col - or T V's._____

⊕ **Coda**

Verse

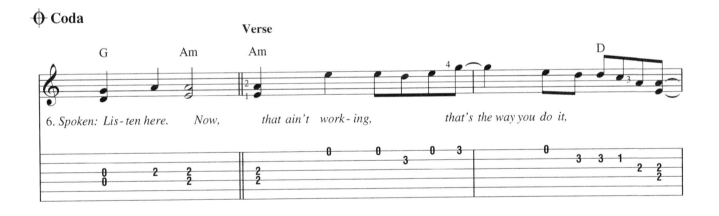

6. *Spoken: Lis - ten here.* *Now,* *that ain't work - ing,* *that's the way you do it,*

you play the gui - tar on the M T V. That ain't __ work - in', that's __

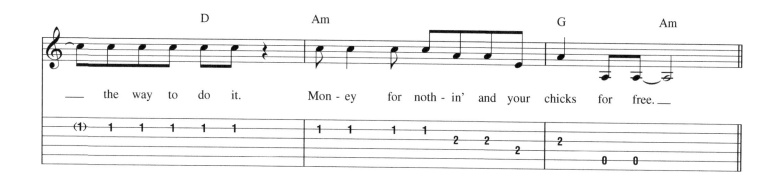

Outro

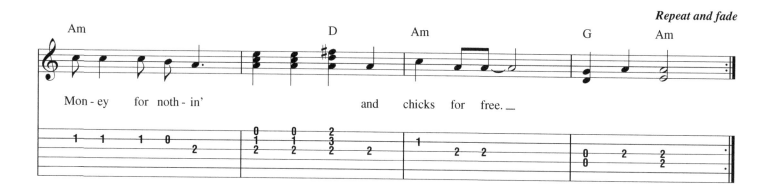

Additional Lyrics

3. The little faggot with the earring and the makeup;
   Yeah, buddy, that's his own hair.
   That little faggot got his own jet airplane.
   That little faggot he's a millionaire.

4. I should a learned to play the guitar.
   I should a learned to play them drums.
   Look at that mama, she got it stickin' in the camera.
   Man we could have some fun.

5. And he's up there. What's that? Hawaiian noises?
   He's bangin' on the bongos like a chimpanzee.
   Oh, that ain't working. That's the way you do it.
   Get your money for nothin', get your chicks for free.

Once Bitten Twice Shy

Words and Music by Ian Hunter

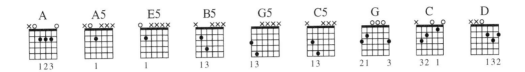

*Capo III

Strum Pattern: 1, 2
Pick Pattern: 1, 2

Intro
Moderate Rock

*Optional: To match recording, place capo at 3rd fret.

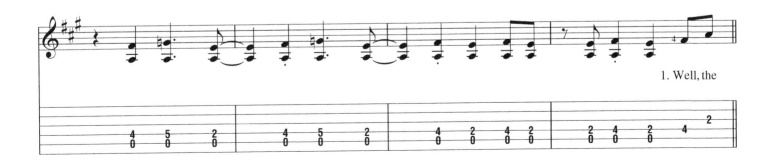

1. Well, the

Copyright © 1975 (Renewed 2003), 1980 EMI APRIL MUSIC INC. and IAN HUNTER MUSIC, INC.
All Rights Controlled and Administered by EMI APRIL MUSIC INC.
All Rights Reserved   International Copyright Secured   Used by Permission

Verse

times are get-ting hard for you, ___ lit-tle girl. I'm a hum-min' and a strum-min' all

o-ver God's world. You can't re-mem-ber when you got your last meal, ___

and you don't know just how ___ a wom-an feels. You did-n't know what

rock 'n' roll was un-til you met my drum-mer on a grey tour ___ bus. ___

I got there in the nick of time ___ be-fore he got his hands a-cross ___

Interlude

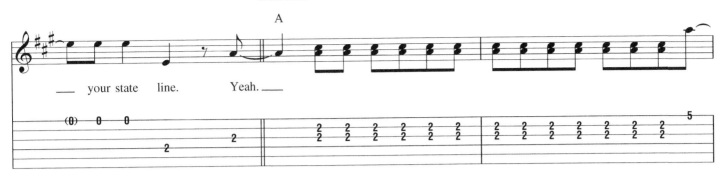

_____ your state   line.   Yeah. _____

% Verse

2. Now it's the   mid - dle   of   the   night _____   on   the
   wom - an,   you're   a   mess, _____   gon - na
4. _Instrumental_

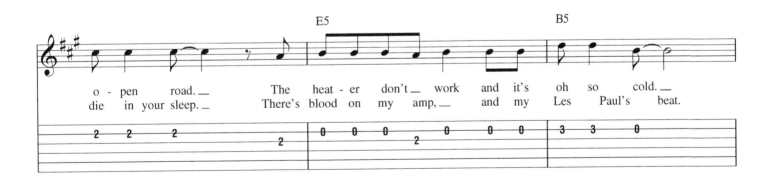

o - pen   road. _____   The   heat - er   don't _____   work   and   it's   oh   so   cold. _____
die   in   your   sleep. _____   There's   blood   on   my   amp, _____   and   my   Les   Paul's   beat.

You're   look - in'   tired,   you're   look - in'   kind - a   beat,   the   rhy - thm   of   the   street   sure   knocks _____
Can't   keep   you   home,   you're   mes - sin'   a - round. _____   My   best   friend   told   me   you're   the

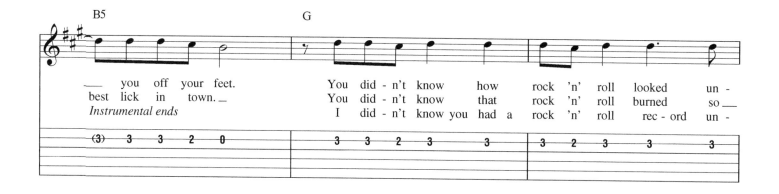

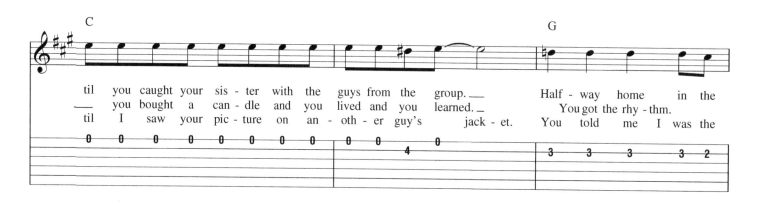

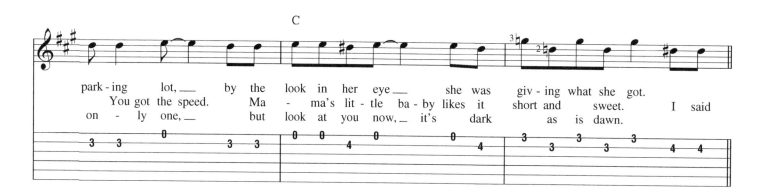

Chorus

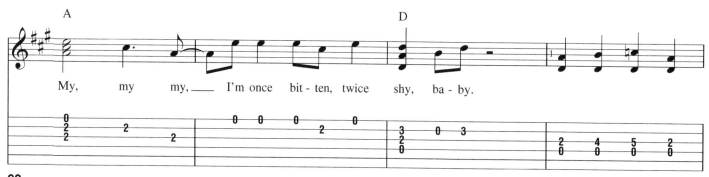

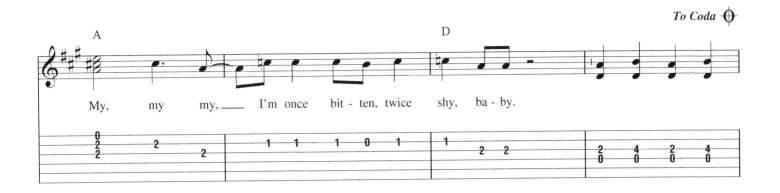

My, my my, ___ I'm once bit - ten, twice shy, ba - by.

|1. ‖ |2.

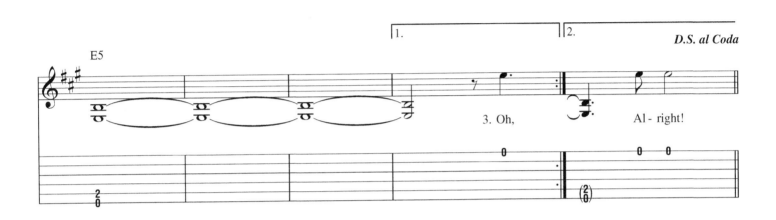

3. Oh,   Al - right!

⊕ **Coda**

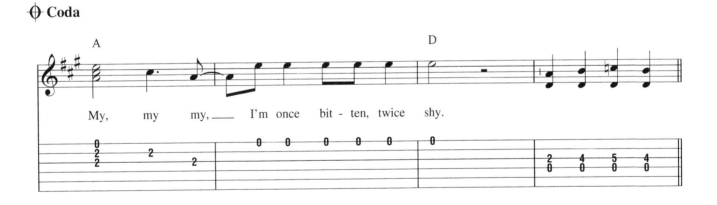

My, my my, ___ I'm once bit - ten, twice shy.

Outro-Guitar Solo

Repeat and fade

Panama

Words and Music by David Lee Roth, Edward Van Halen, Alex Van Halen and Michael Anthony

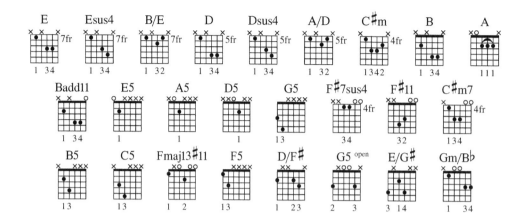

*Tune down 1/2 step:
(low to high) Eb-Ab-Db-Gb-Bb-Eb

Strum Pattern: 1, 4
Pick Pattern: 2, 4
   Intro
     Moderate Rock

*Optional: To match recording, tune down 1/2 step.

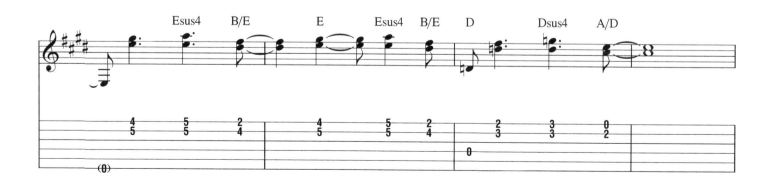

Copyright © 1984 Diamond Dave Music, WB Music Corp. and Van Halen Music
All Rights for Diamond Dave Music Administered by Red Stripe Plane Music, LLC
All Rights for Van Halen Music Administered by WB Music Corp.
All Rights Reserved   Used by Permission

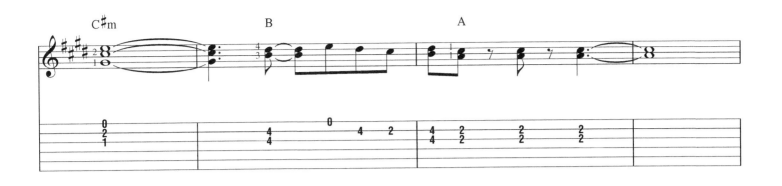

Verse

1. Jump back. What's that sound? ___
2. *See additional lyrics*

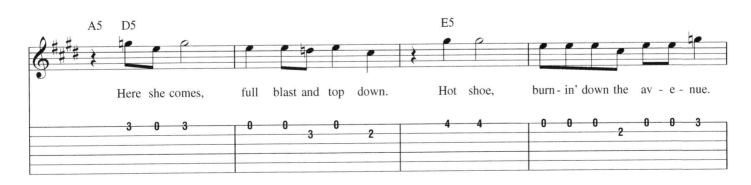

Here she comes, full blast and top down. Hot shoe, burn-in' down the av-e-nue.

Pre-Chorus

A5   E5   F#7sus4

Mod - el cit - i - zen,   ze - ro dis - ci - pline.   Don't you know she's com - in'

F#11   C#m7

home _ to me? _____   You'll lose her in the turn. _   *Spoken: I'll get her.

*Lyrics in italics are
spoken throughout.

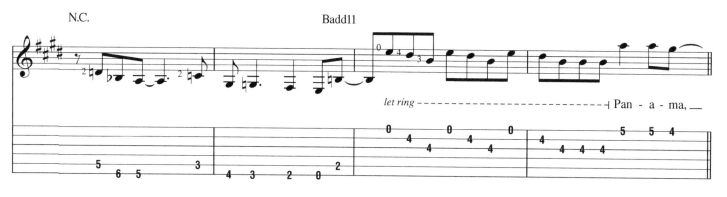

N.C.   Badd11

let ring ----------------------------| Pan - a - ma, _

Chorus

E5 A5 D5   A5   D5 A5 G5   E5 A5 D5   A5   D5 A5 G5

_   Pan - a - ma. _____   Pan - a - ma, _

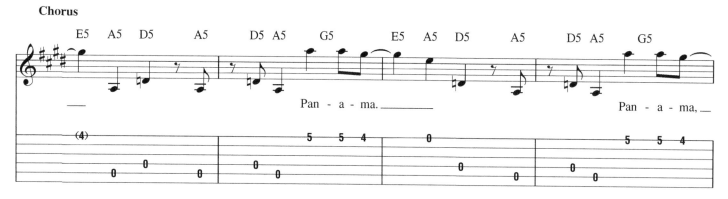

1.

E5 A5 D5   A5   D5 A5 G5   E5 A5 D5   A5   D5 A5 G5

_   Pan - a - ma. _____

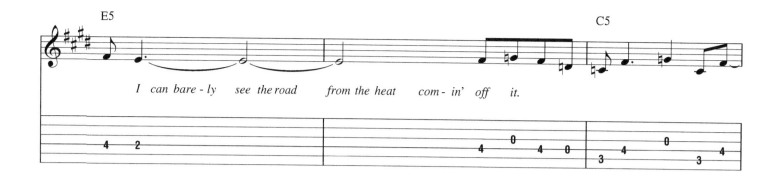

I can bare - ly see the road from the heat com - in' off it.

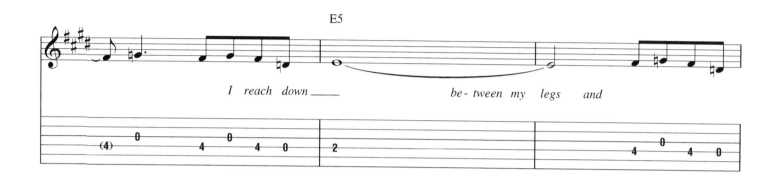

I reach down _____ be - tween my legs and

ease the seat _____ back. She's blind - in',

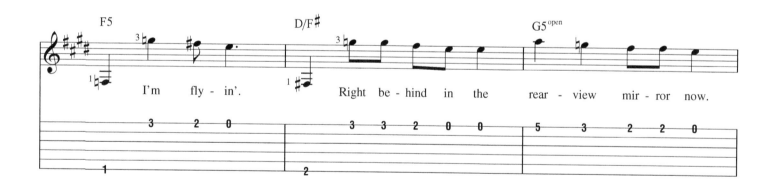

I'm fly - in'. Right be - hind in the rear - view mir - ror now.

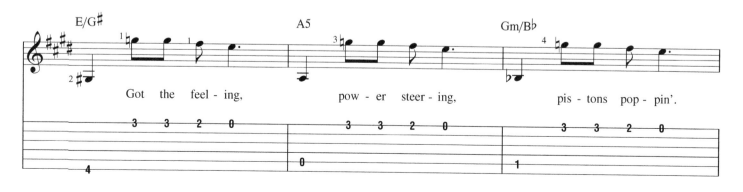

Got the feel - ing, pow - er steer - ing, pis - tons pop - pin'.

Chorus

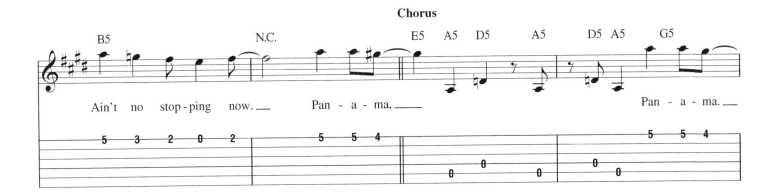

Ain't no stop-ping now. ___ Pan - a - ma, ___ Pan - a - ma. ___

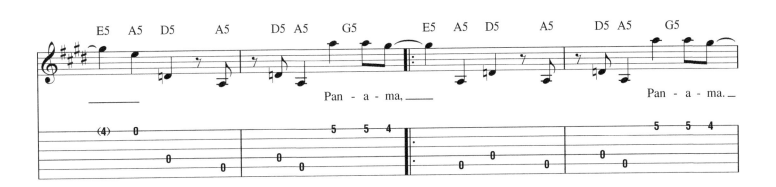

Pan - a - ma, ___ Pan - a - ma. ___

Pan - a - ma, ___ Pan - a - ma. ___

Additional Lyrics

2. Ain't nothin' like it, her shiny machine,
   Got the feel for the wheel, keep the moving parts clean.
   Hot shoe, burnin' down the avenue,
   Got an on-ramp comin' through my bedroom.

Seventeen

Words and Music by Kip Winger, Reb Beach and Beau Hill

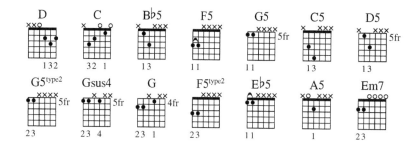

*Drop D tuning, capo I:
(low to high) D-A-D-G-B-E

Strum Pattern: 3
Pick Pattern: 4

Intro
Moderate Rock

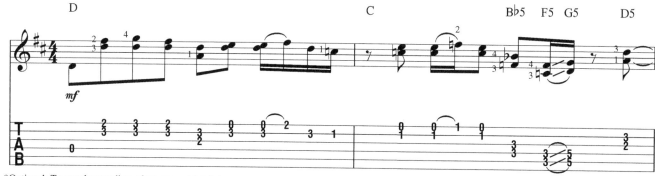

*Optional: To match recording, place capo at 1st fret.

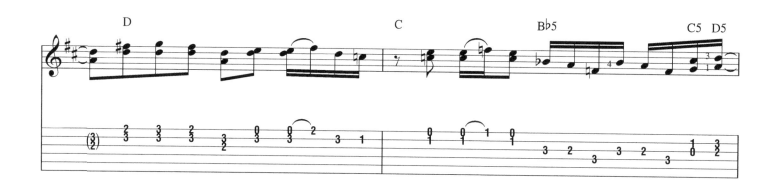

Copyright © 1988 EMI VIRGIN SONGS, INC., VARSEAU MUSIC, INC., SMALL HOPE MUSIC LTD.,
EMI VIRGIN MUSIC, INC., JULIAN KELLY MUSIC and BLUE 32 MUSIC
All Rights for VARSEAU MUSIC, INC. and SMALL HOPE MUSIC LTD. Controlled and Administered by EMI VIRGIN SONGS, INC.
All Rights for JULIAN KELLY MUSIC and BLUE 32 MUSIC Controlled and Administered by EMI VIRGIN MUSIC, INC.
All Rights Reserved   International Copyright Secured   Used by Permission

Verse

*Sung one octave higher, next 8 meas.

To Coda

Pre-Chorus

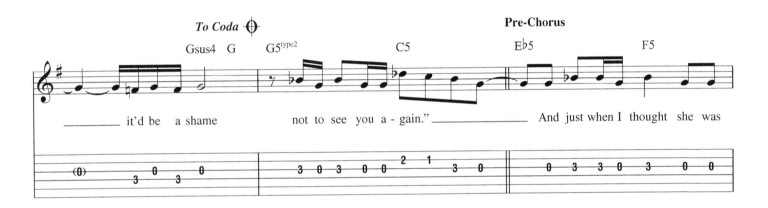

Chorus

*Sung as written throughout Chorus.

like you've nev - er seen."
ain't seen noth - in' like me."
She's on - ly sev - en - teen.____ (Sev - en - teen.)

Dad - dy says she's too young, but she's old e - nough for me. ____

Guitar Solo

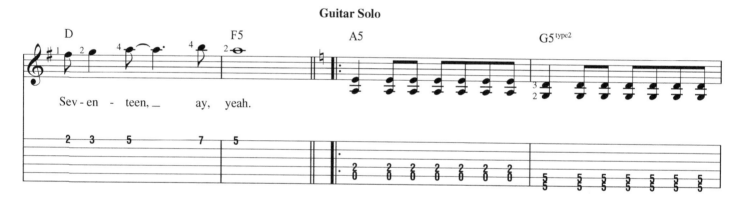

Sev - en - teen, __ ay, yeah.

Interlude

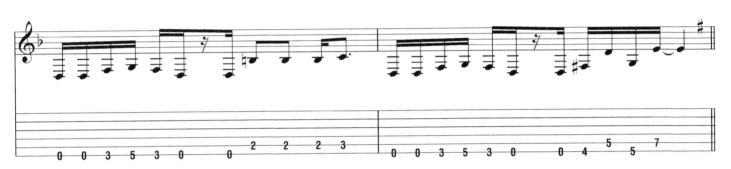

D.S. al Coda

Coda   **Outro-Chorus**

It   must   be   love._____
me._____   Yeah,   yeah._

She's   on - ly   sev - en -   teen._

*Sung as written till fade.

___   (Sev - en - teen.)__   That   girl,   she   gives   me   love   like   I've   nev - er   seen."
___   Yeah, yeah.   *2nd time, Instrumental till fade*

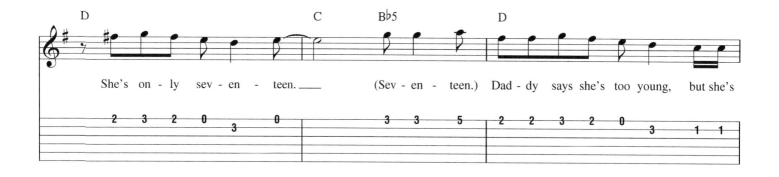

She's on - ly sev - en - teen. ____ (Sev - en - teen.) Dad - dy says she's too young, but she's

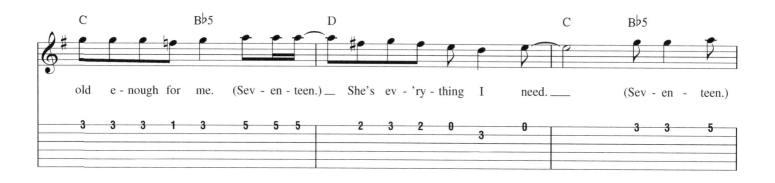

old e - nough for me. (Sev - en - teen.) ___ She's ev - 'ry - thing I need. ____ (Sev - en - teen.)

Repeat and fade

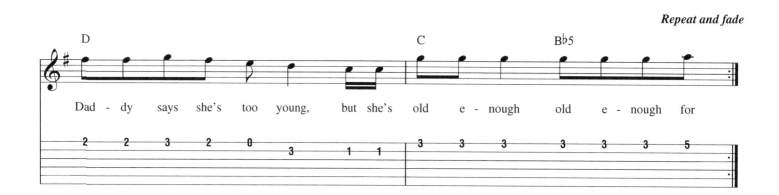

Dad - dy says she's too young, but she's old e - nough old e - nough for

Additional Lyrics

2. Mm, come to my place; we can talk it over,
   Oh, ev'rything going down in your head.
   She says, "Take it easy, I need some time.
   Time to work it out, to make you mine."

3. Yeah, such a bad girl, loves to work me overtime.
   Feels good, hah, dancing close to the borderline.
   She's a magic mountain, she's a leather glove.
   Oh, she's my soul. It must be love.

Should I Stay or Should I Go

Words and Music by Mick Jones and Joe Strummer

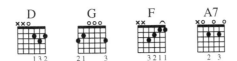

Strum Pattern: 6
Pick Pattern: 5

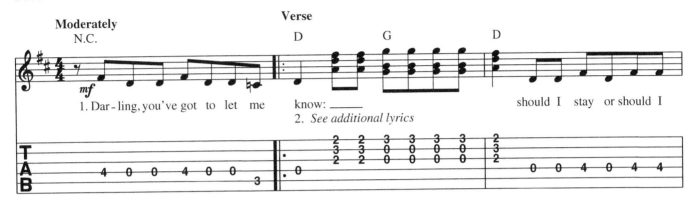

1. Dar-ling, you've got to let me know: _____ should I stay or should I
2. *See additional lyrics*

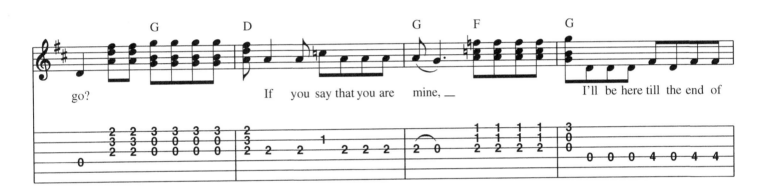

go? If you say that you are mine, — I'll be here till the end of

time. So you've got to let me know: _ should I stay or should I

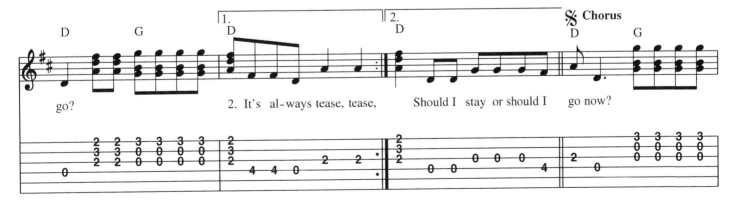

go? 2. It's al-ways tease, tease, Should I stay or should I go now?

Copyright © 1982 NINEDEN LTD.
All Rights in the U.S. and Canada Controlled and Administered by UNIVERSAL - POLYGRAM INTERNATIONAL PUBLISHING, INC.
All Rights Reserved   Used by Permission

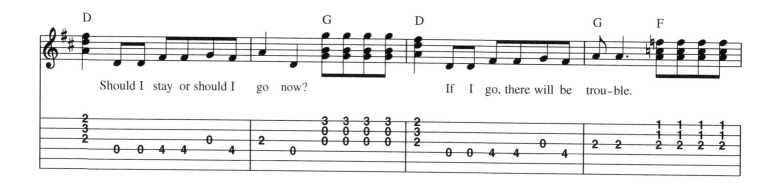

Should I stay or should I go now? If I go, there will be trou-ble.

To Coda ⊕

And if I stay, it will be dou-ble. So you've got to let me know: —

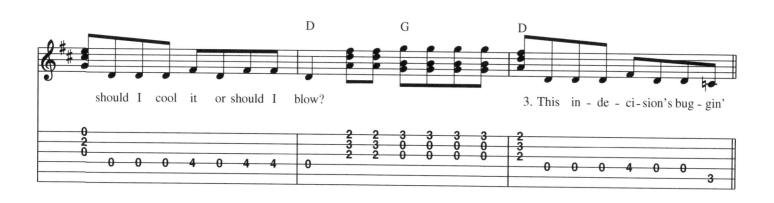

should I cool it or should I blow? 3. This in-de-ci-sion's bug-gin'

Verse

me. If you don't want me set me free. Ex-act-ly who'm I s'posed to

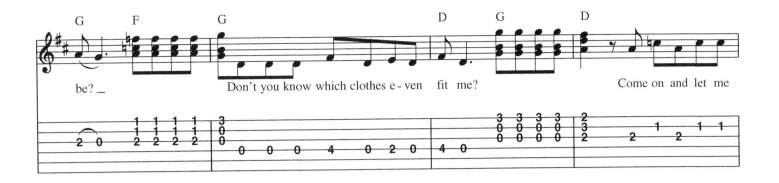

be?— Don't you know which clothes e-ven fit me? Come on and let me

D.S. al Coda

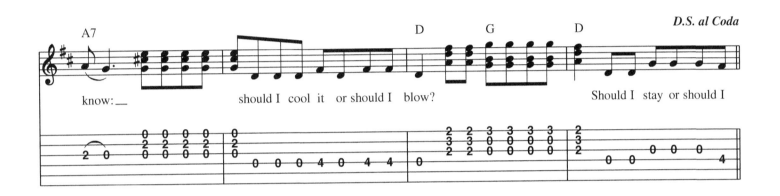

know:— should I cool it or should I blow? Should I stay or should I

⊕ **Coda**

should I stay or should I go?

Additional Lyrics

2. It's always tease, tease, tease.
   You're happy when I'm on my knees.
   One day is fine and next is black.
   So if you want me off your back,
   Well, come on and let me know:
   Should I stay or should I go?

Sharp Dressed Man

Words and Music by Billy F Gibbons, Dusty Hill and Frank Lee Beard

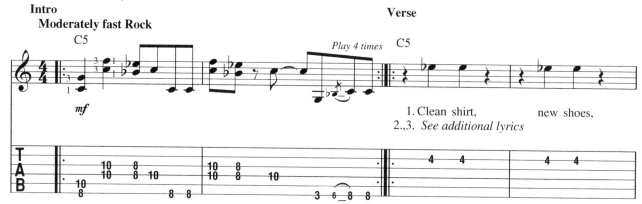

Strum Pattern: 1, 2

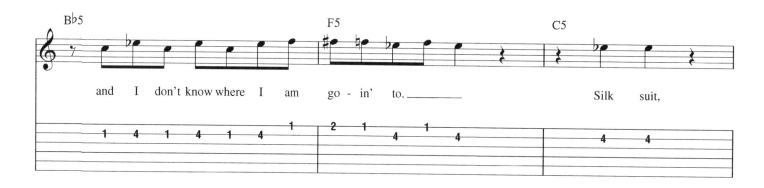

Copyright © 1983 Music Of Stage Three
All Rights Administered by Stage Three Music (U.S.) Inc.
All Rights Reserved   Used by Permission

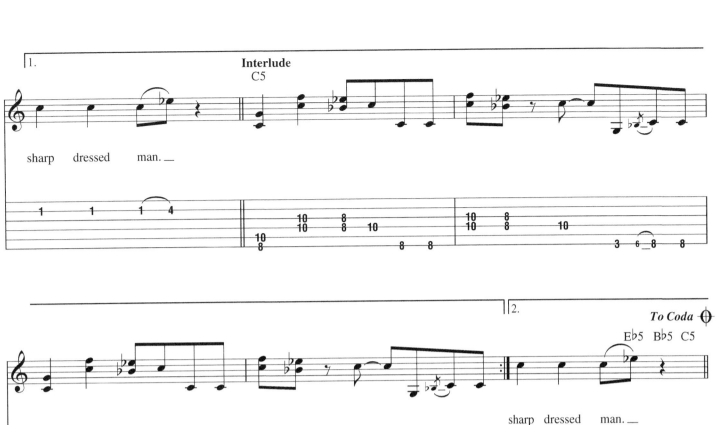

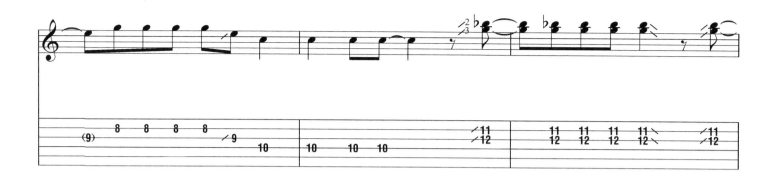

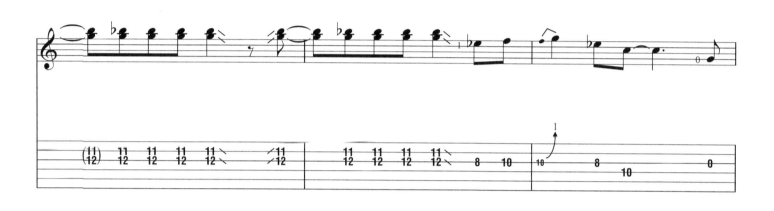

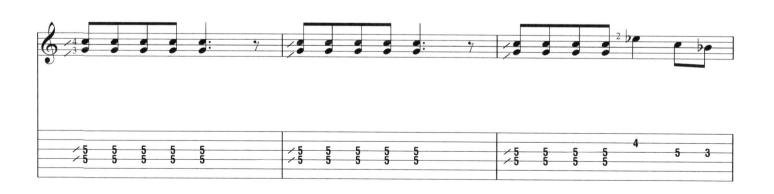

Additional Lyrics

2. Gold watch, diamond ring,
   I ain't missin' not a single thing.
   Cuff links, stick pin,
   When I step out I'm gonna do you in.
   They come runnin' just as fast as they can,
   'Cause every girl crazy 'bout a sharp dressed man.

3. Top coat, top hat,
   I don't worry 'cause my wallet's fat.
   Black shades, white gloves,
   Lookin' sharp, lookin' for love.
   They come runnin' just as fast as they can,
   'Cause every girl crazy 'bout a sharp dressed man.

Stray Cat Strut

Words and Music by Brian Setzer

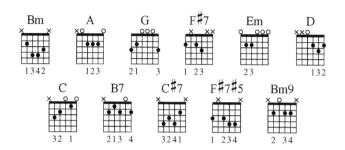

*Capo I

Strum Pattern: 4, 5
Pick Pattern: 1, 3

Intro
Moderately

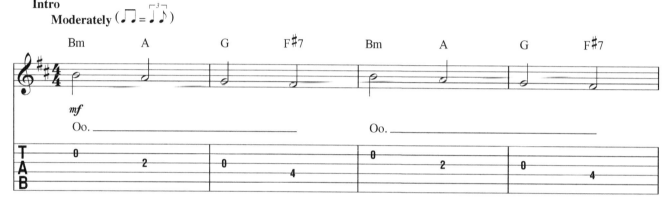

Oo. _____ Oo. _____

*Optional: To match recording, place capo at 1st fret.

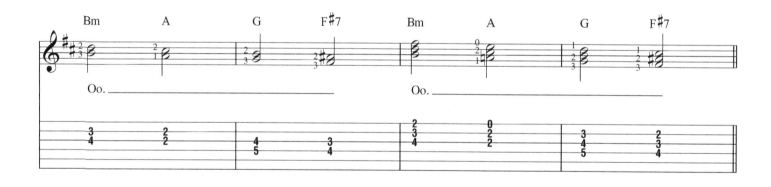

Oo. _____ Oo. _____

Verse

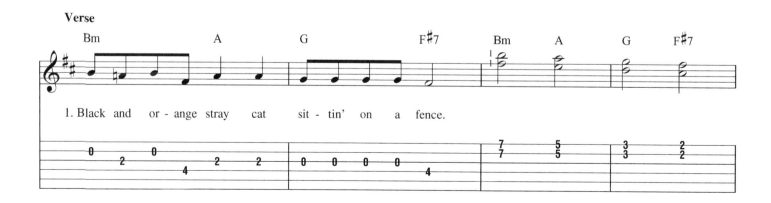

1. Black and or-ange stray cat sit-tin' on a fence.

Copyright © 1981 EMI LONGITUDE MUSIC and ROCKIN' BONES MUSIC
All Rights Controlled and Administered by EMI LONGITUDE MUSIC
All Rights Reserved International Copyright Secured Used by Permission

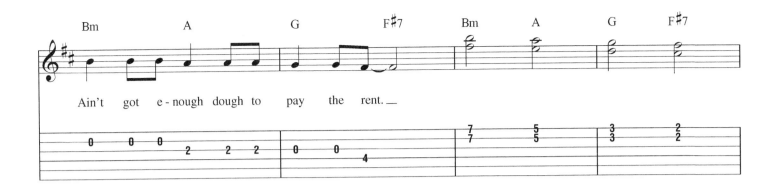

Ain't got e-nough dough to pay the rent.

I'm flat broke, but I don't care, _ I strut right by with my tail in the air.

Chorus

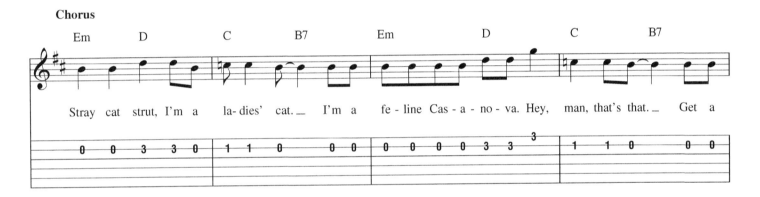

Stray cat strut, I'm a la-dies' cat. _ I'm a fe-line Cas-a-no-va. Hey, man, that's that. _ Get a

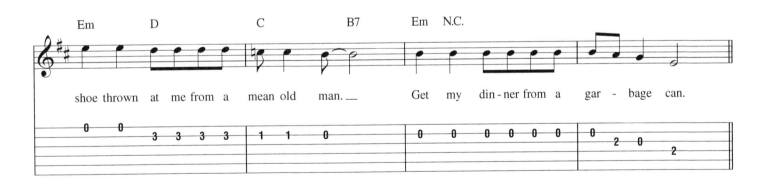

shoe thrown at me from a mean old man. _ Get my din-ner from a gar-bage can.

Interlude

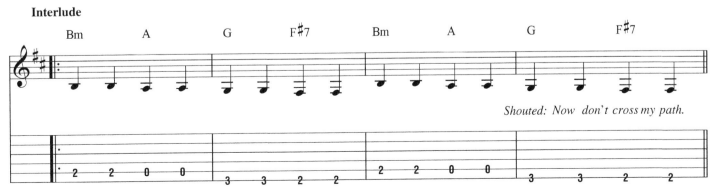

Shouted: Now don't cross my path.

Guitar Solo

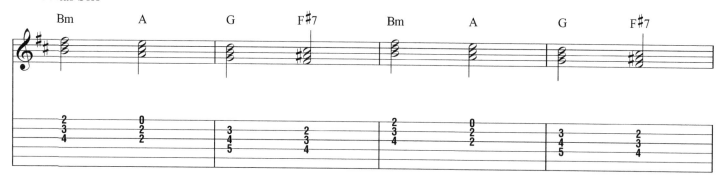

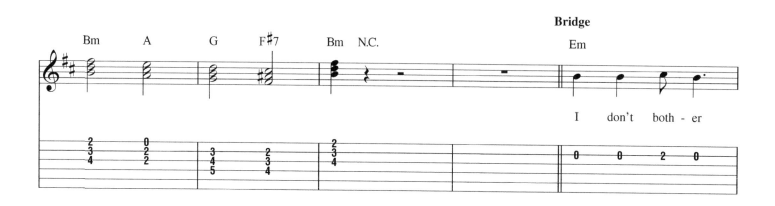

Bridge

I don't both - er

chas - in' mice a - round. ___ Whoa, no. ___ I slink down the al - ley,

look - in' for a fight, howl - in' to the moon - light on a hot sum - mer night. ___

Verse

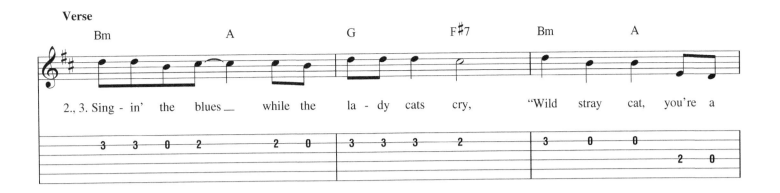

2., 3. Sing - in' the blues __ while the la - dy cats cry, "Wild stray cat, you're a

real gone guy." I wish I could be as care - free and wild, __ but I

Outro

got cat class and I got class style.

Summer of '69

Words and Music by Bryan Adams and Jim Vallance

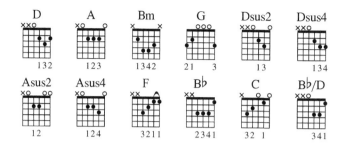

Strum Pattern: 1, 6
Pick Pattern: 3, 4

Intro
Moderately fast Rock

Verse

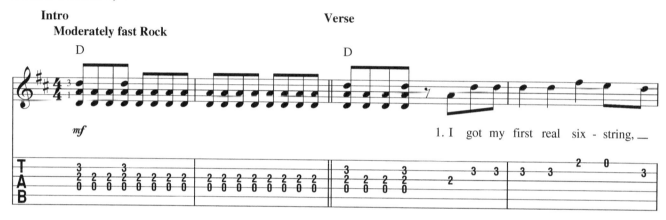

1. I got my first real six - string, __

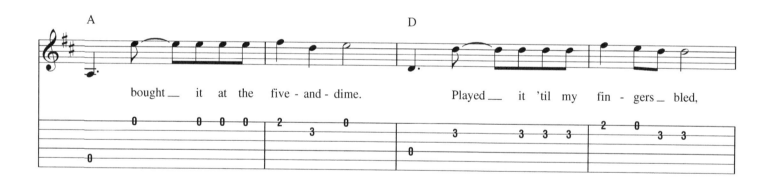

bought __ it at the five - and - dime. Played __ it 'til my fin - gers __ bled,

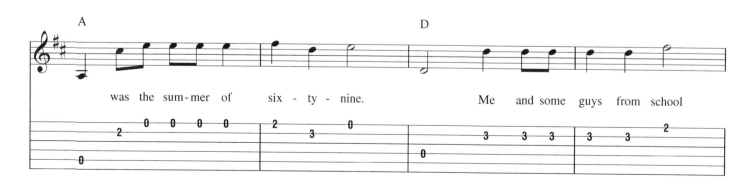

was the sum-mer of six - ty - nine. Me and some guys from school

Copyright © 1984 IRVING MUSIC, INC., ADAMS COMMUNICATIONS, INC., ALMO MUSIC CORP. and TESTATYME MUSIC
All Rights for ADAMS COMMUNICATIONS, INC. Controlled and Administered by IRVING MUSIC, INC.
All Rights for TESTATYME MUSIC Controlled and Administered by ALMO MUSIC CORP.
All Rights Reserved   Used by Permission

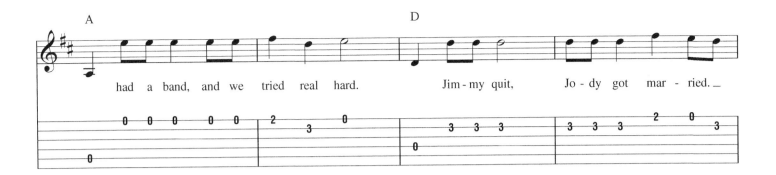

had a band, and we tried real hard. Jim-my quit, Jo - dy got mar - ried. _

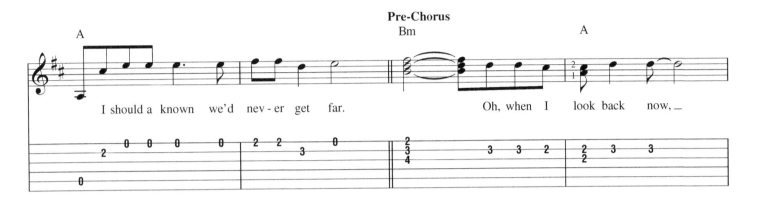

Pre-Chorus

I should a known we'd nev - er get far. Oh, when I look back now, _

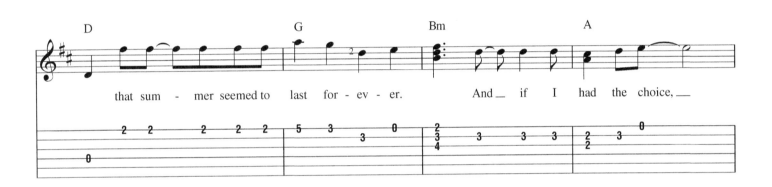

that sum - mer seemed to last for - ev - er. And _ if I had the choice, _

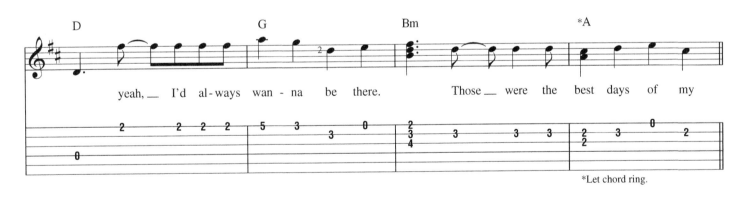

yeah, _ I'd al - ways wan - na be there. Those _ were the best days of my

*Let chord ring.

Chorus

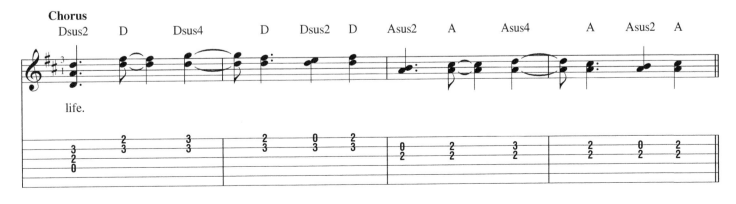

life.

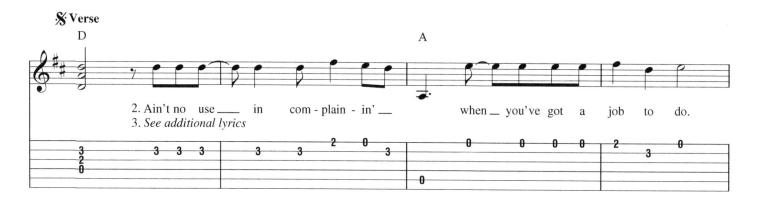

Verse

2. Ain't no use ___ in com - plain - in' ___ when ___ you've got a job to do.
3. *See additional lyrics*

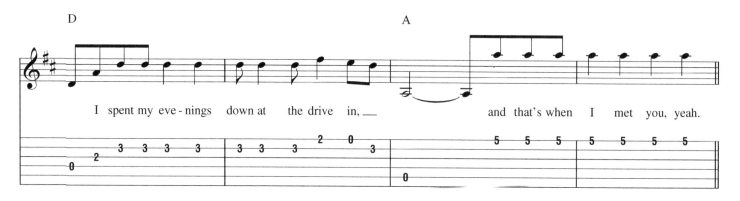

I spent my eve - nings down at the drive in, ___ and that's when I met you, yeah.

Pre-Chorus

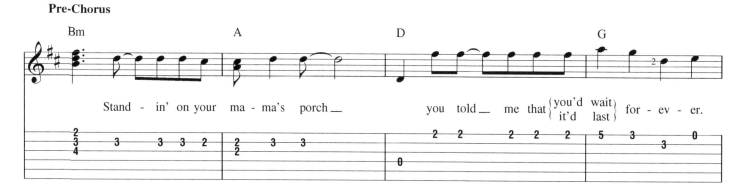

Stand - in' on your ma - ma's porch ___ you told ___ me that { you'd wait / it'd last } for - ev - er.

Oh, ___ and when you held my hand, ___ I knew ___ that it was now or nev - er.

Chorus

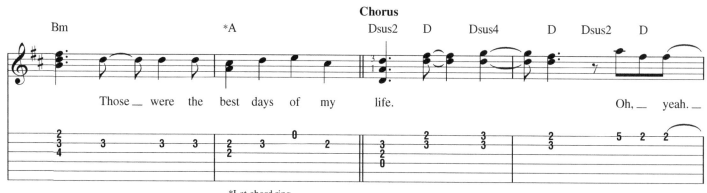

Those ___ were the best days of my life. Oh, ___ yeah. ___

*Let chord ring.

118

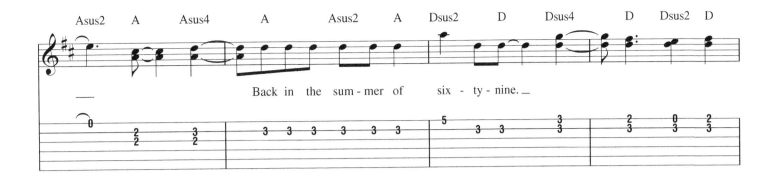

Back in the sum - mer of six - ty - nine. ____

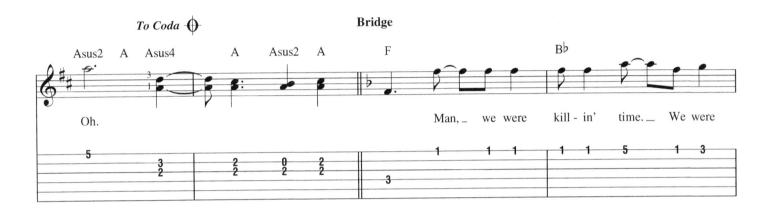

Oh.

Man, ____ we were kill - in' time. ____ We were

young and rest - less, we need - ed to un - wind.

I guess noth - in' can last ____ for -

ev - er, for - ev - er. No!

2nd time, D.S. al Coda

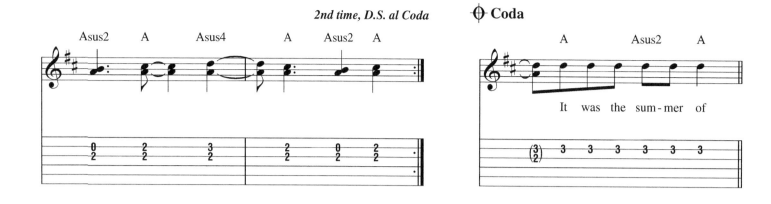

Coda

It was the sum-mer of

Outro

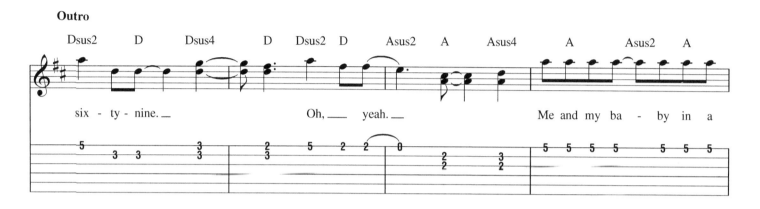

six - ty - nine. ___ Oh, ___ yeah. ___ Me and my ba - by in a

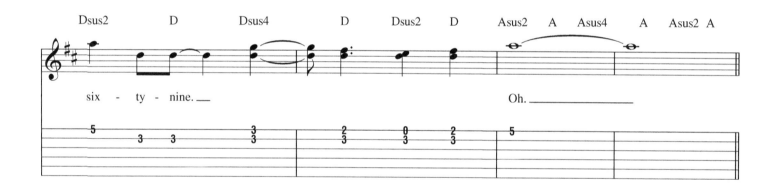

six - ty - nine. ___ Oh. ___

Repeat and fade

Additional Lyrics

3. And now the times are changin'.
Look at everything that's come and gone.
Sometimes when I play that old six-string,
I think about you, wonder what went wrong.

Talk Dirty to Me

Words and Music by Bobby Dall, Brett Michaels, Bruce Johannesson and Rikki Rockett

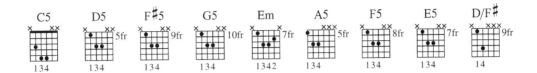

*Tune down 1/2 step:
(low to high) Eb-Ab-Db-Gb-Bb-Eb

Strum Pattern: 1, 2
Pick Pattern: 4

Intro
Moderate Rock

*Optional: To match recording, tune down 1/2 step.

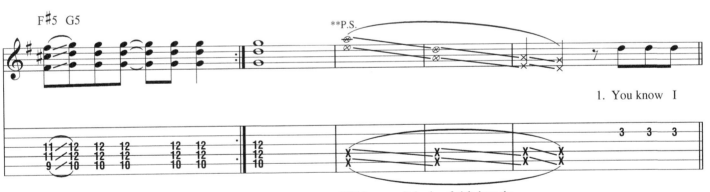

**Pick scrape: Rub edge of pick down the
strings, producing a scratchy sound.

1. You know I

Verse

nev-er, I nev-er seen you look so good, _ you nev-er act the way you should, _

Copyright © 1987 by Cyanide Publishing
All Rights in the United States Administered by Universal Music - Z Songs
International Copyright Secured   All Rights Reserved

Verse

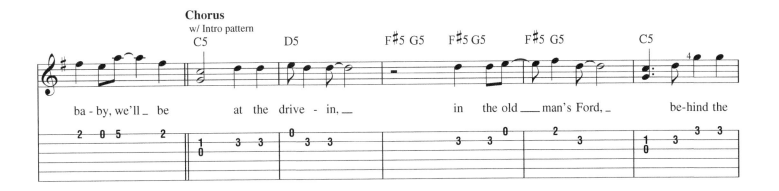

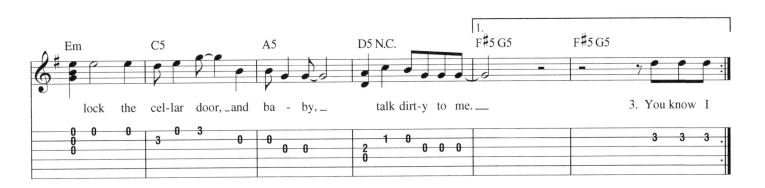

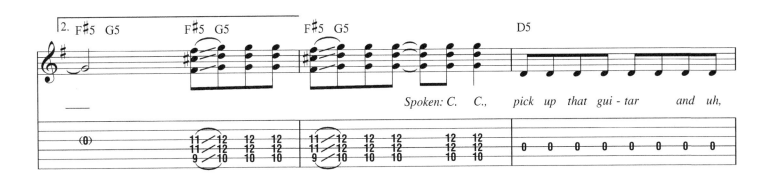

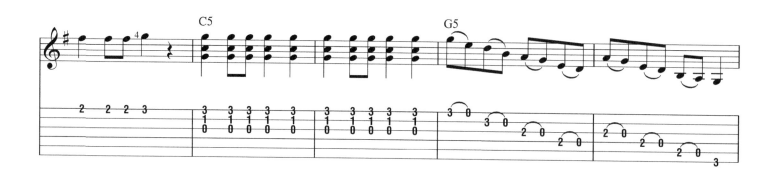

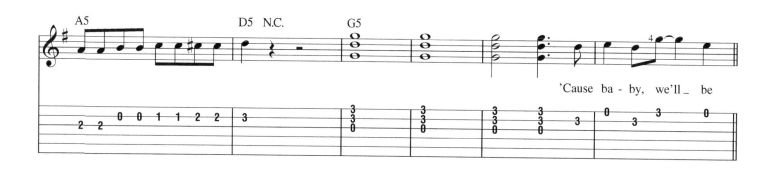

'Cause ba - by, we'll _ be

Chorus
w/ Intro pattern

at the drive - in, _ in the old _ man's Ford, _ be-hind them bush-es,

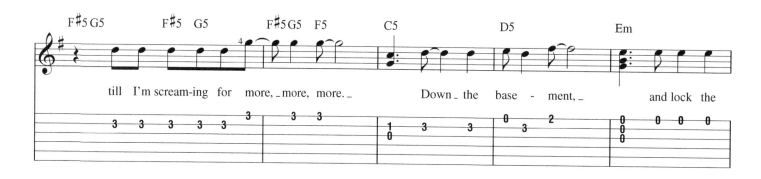

till I'm scream-ing for more, _ more, more. _ Down _ the base - ment, _ and lock the

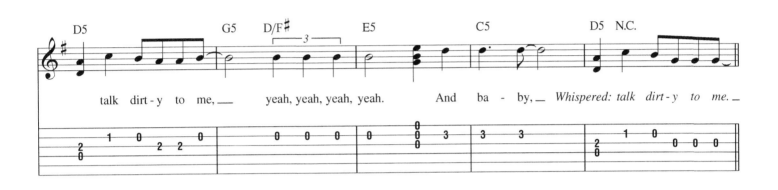

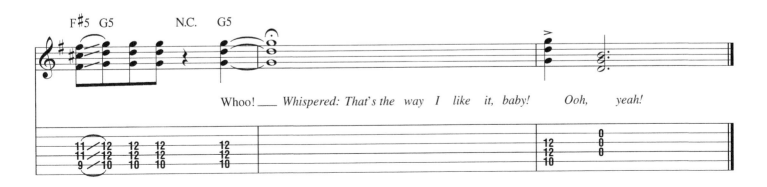

We're Not Gonna Take It

Words and Music by Daniel Dee Snider

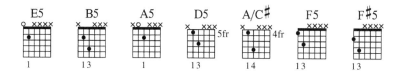

Strum Pattern: 1, 2

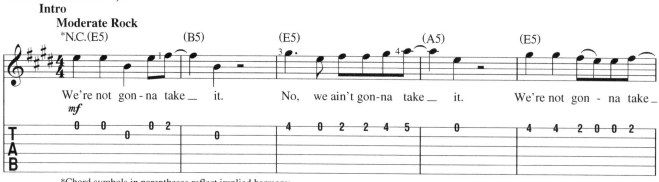

*Chord symbols in parentheses reflect implied harmony.

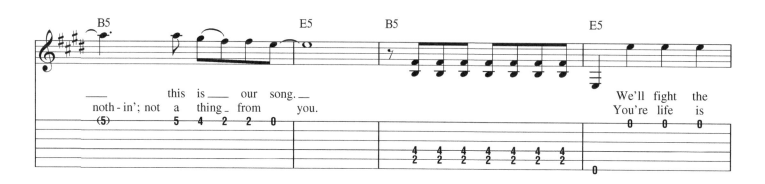

Copyright © 1984 by Universal Music - Z Melodies and Snidest Music
All Rights in the United States Administered by Universal Music - Z Melodies
International Copyright Secured   All Rights Reserved

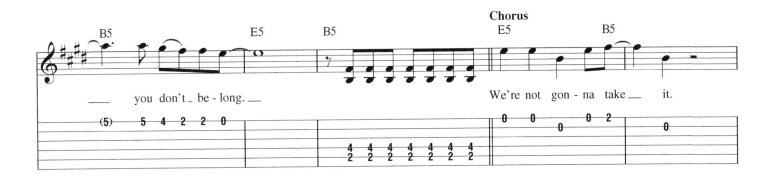

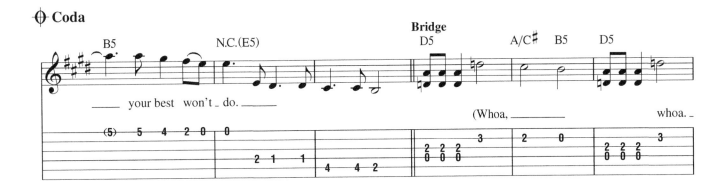

Chorus

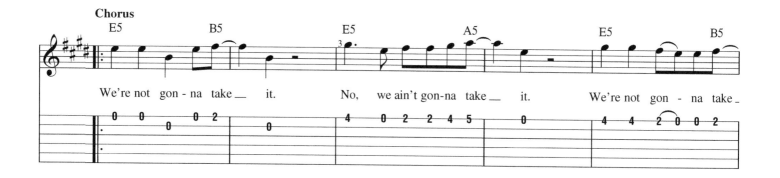

We're not gon - na take __ it. No, we ain't gon-na take __ it. We're not gon - na take __

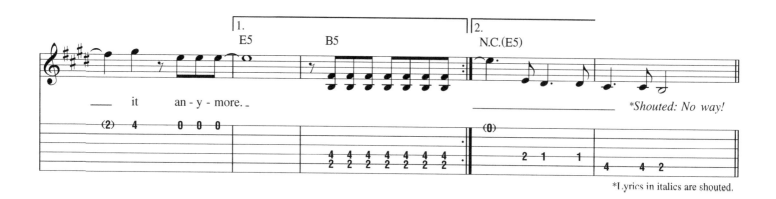

__ it an - y - more. __

Shouted: No way!

*Lyrics in italics are shouted.

Guitar Solo

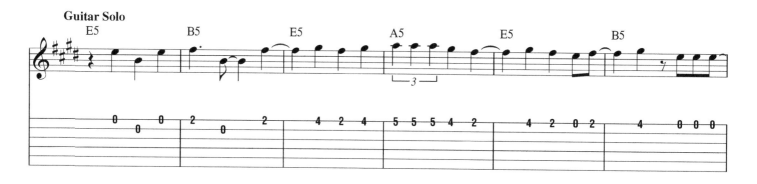

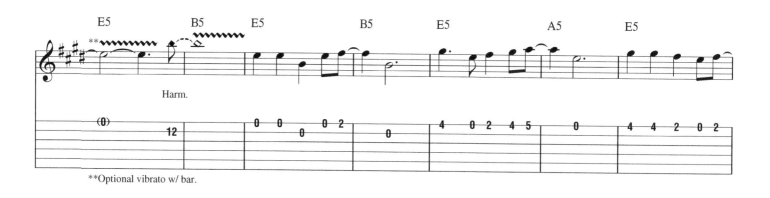

Harm.

**Optional vibrato w/ bar.

Bridge

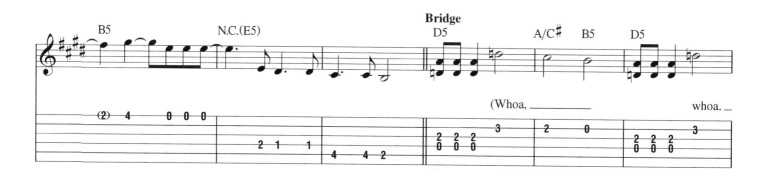

(Whoa, _____ whoa. __

128

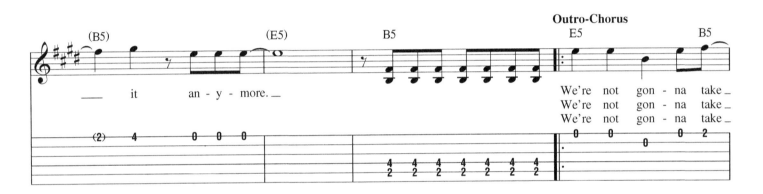

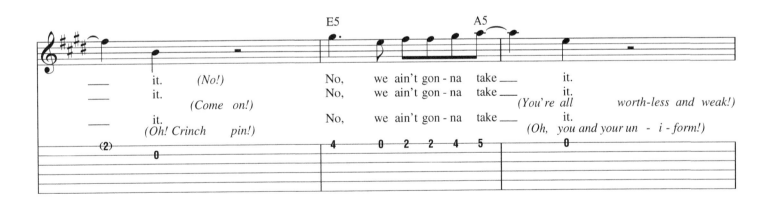

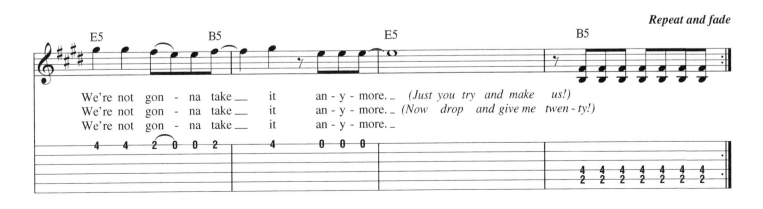

White Wedding

Words and Music by Billy Idol

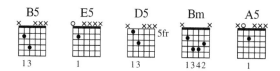

Strum Pattern: 1

Intro
Moderately fast Rock

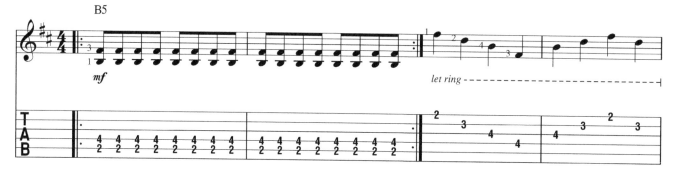

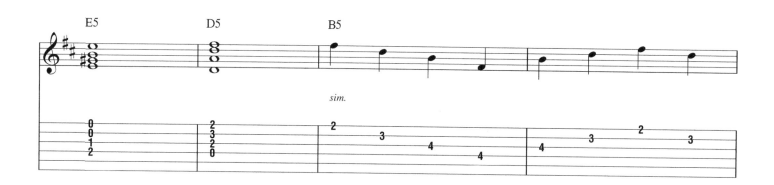

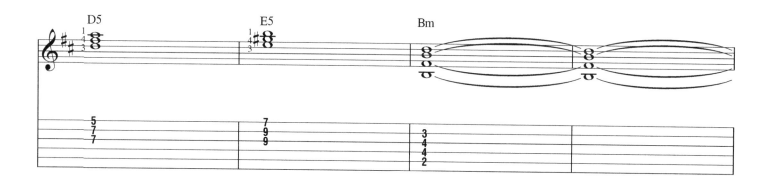

Copyright © 1982 Chrysalis Music and Boneidol Music
All Rights Administered by Chrysalis Music
All Rights Reserved   Used by Permission

Verse

1. Hey, lit-tle sis-ter, what have you done? _____
2., 3. *See additional lyrics*

Hey, lit-tle sis-ter, who's _ the on - ly one? _____

Hey, lit-tle sis-ter, who's _ your su - per - man?

Hey, lit-tle sis-ter, who's _ the one _ you want? Hey, lit-tle sis-ter, shot - gun! It's a

Chorus

nice day to start _ a - gain. _____

1., 2. It's a
3. Come on, it's a

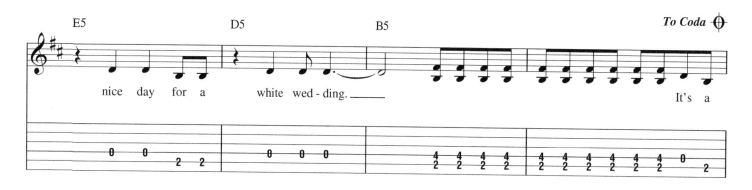

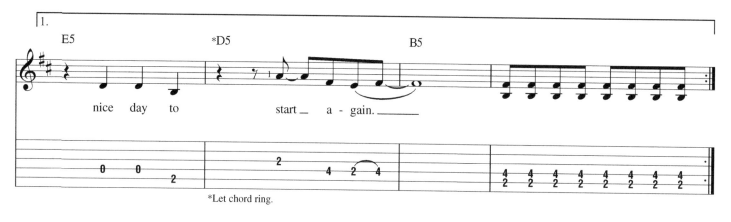

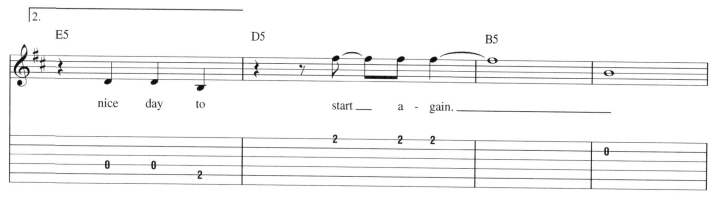

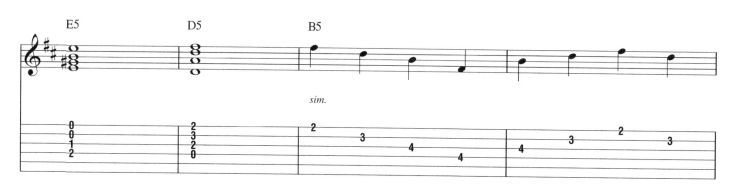

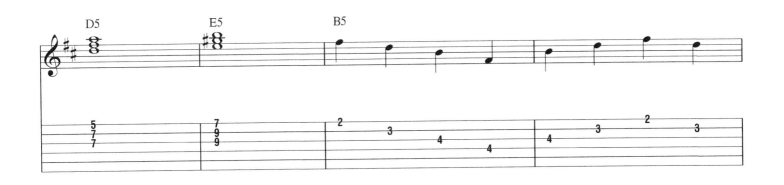

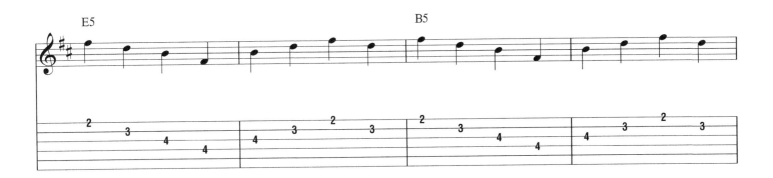

Spoken: Pick it up.

D.S. al Coda

Take __ me back home, yeah.

✛ Coda

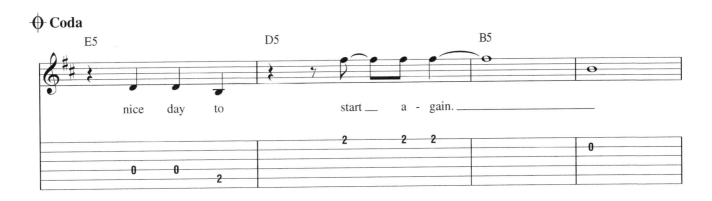

nice   day   to   start __ a - gain. _____

Bridge

Outro-Chorus

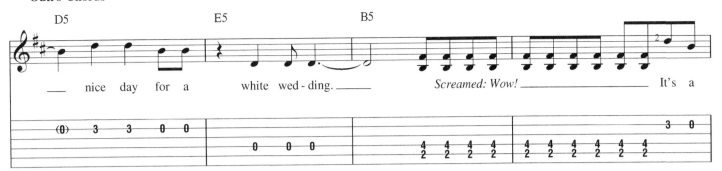

__ nice day for a   white wed - ding. _____   *Screamed: Wow!* _____ It's a

nice day to   start __ a - gain. _____   It's a

Repeat and fade

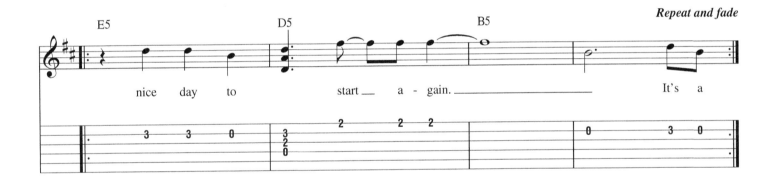

nice day to   start __ a - gain. _____   It's a

Additional Lyrics

2. Hey little sister, who is it you're with?
   Hey little sister, what's your fascination?
   Hey little sister, shotgun, oh, yeah.
   Hey little sister, who's your superman?
   Hey little sister, shotgun!

3. Hey little sister, what have you done?
   Hey little sister, who's the only one?
   I've been away for so long.
   I've been away for so long.
   I let you go for so long.

Working for the Weekend

Words and Music by Paul Dean, Matthew Frenette and Michael Reno

© 1981 EMI APRIL MUSIC (CANADA) LTD., DEAN OF MUSIC, EMI BLACKWOOD MUSIC INC. and DUKE RENO MUSIC
All Rights in the U.S.A. Controlled and Administered by EMI APRIL MUSIC INC. and EMI BLACKWOOD MUSIC INC.
All Rights Reserved   International Copyright Secured   Used by Permission

will you come out to-night? _____ Ev - 'ry-one's try -

- in' to get it right, ___ get it right. _____

Chorus

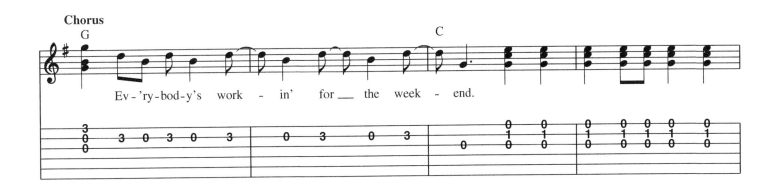

Ev - 'ry-bod-y's work - in' for __ the week - end.

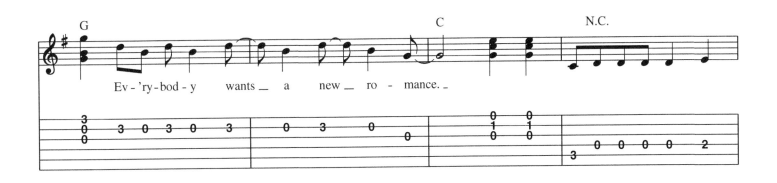

Ev - 'ry-bod-y wants __ a new __ ro - mance. __

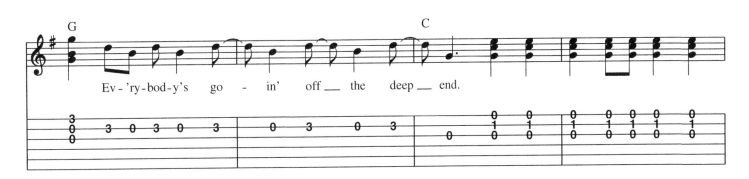

Ev - 'ry-bod-y's go - in' off __ the deep __ end.

Ev - 'ry - bod - y needs ___ a sec - ond chance, ___ oh. _____

Bridge

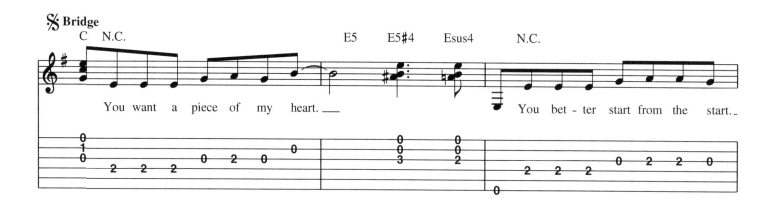

You want a piece of my heart. ___ You bet - ter start from the start. ___

___ You wan - na be in the show. ___

Interlude

Come on, ba - by, let's go! ___

To Coda ⊕

Additional Lyrics

2. Ev'ryone's lookin' to see if it was you.
   Ev'ryone wants you to come through.
   Ev'ryone's hopin' it'll all work out.
   Ev'ryone's waitin' to hold it out.

You Give Love a Bad Name

Words and Music by Jon Bon Jovi, Desmond Child and Richie Sambora

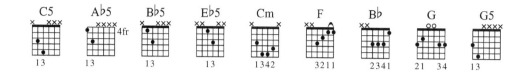

Strum Pattern: 5, 6

Intro
Moderately

Shot through the heart, and you're to blame, dar-lin' you give love a

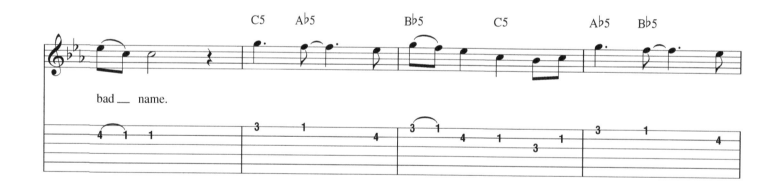

bad name.

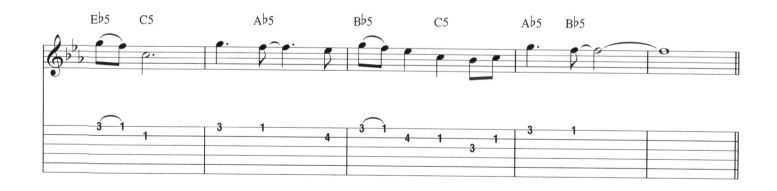

Copyright © 1986 UNIVERSAL - POLYGRAM INTERNATIONAL PUBLISHING, INC., BON JOVI PUBLISHING,
SONY/ATV MUSIC PUBLISHING LLC and AGGRESSIVE MUSIC
All Rights for BON JOVI PUBLISHING Controlled and Administered by UNIVERSAL - POLYGRAM INTERNATIONAL PUBLISHING, INC.
All Rights for SONY/ATV MUSIC PUBLISHING LLC and AGGRESSIVE MUSIC Administered by SONY/ATV MUSIC PUBLISHING LLC,
8 Music Square West, Nashville, TN 37203
All Rights Reserved   Used by Permission

Verse

1. An an-gel's smile ___ is what you sell. You prom-ised me heav-en, then
2. *See additional lyrics*

put me through hell. ___ Chains of ___ love ___ got a hold on me. When

Pre-Chorus

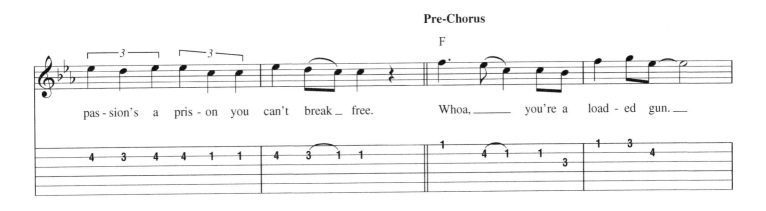

pas-sion's a pris-on you can't break ___ free. Whoa, ___ you're a load-ed gun. ___

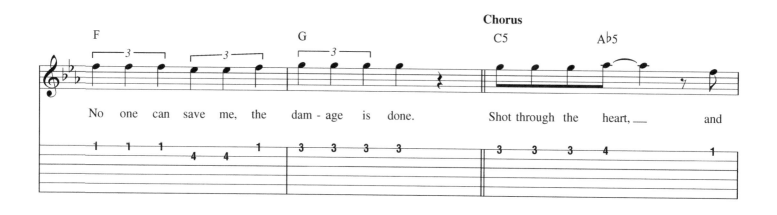

*Let chord ring.

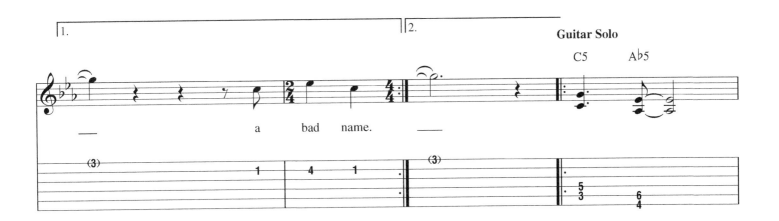

a bad name.

Guitar Solo

C5　A♭5

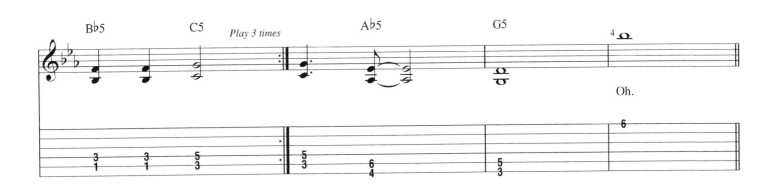

B♭5　C5　*Play 3 times*　A♭5　G5

Oh.

Chorus

N.C.

Shot through the heart, ___ and you're to ___ blame. You give love ___ a

bad name. I play my part, ___ and you play your ___ game. You give love ___ a

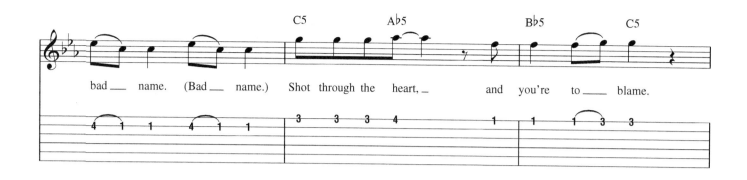

bad ___ name. (Bad ___ name.) Shot through the heart, __ and you're to ___ blame.

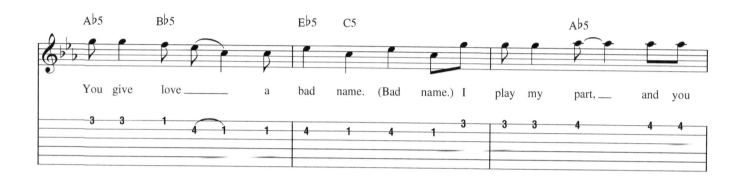

You give love _____ a bad name. (Bad name.) I play my part, __ and you

play your ___ game. You give love _____ a bad name. (Bad name.)

Outro

Repeat and fade

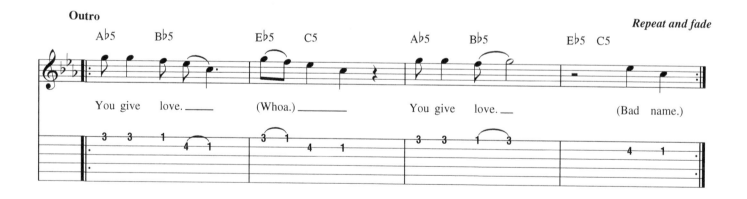

You give love. _____ (Whoa.) _____ You give love. __ (Bad name.)

Additional Lyrics

2. You paint your smile on your lips,
Blood-red nails on your fingertips.
A school boy's dream, you act so shy.
Your very first kiss was your first kiss goodbye.